KU-193-799

JUNGLE RIVERS & MOUNTAIN PEAKS

DISCOVERY AND EXPLORATION

International Learning Systems Corporation Limited · London

JUNGLE RIVERS & MOUNTAIN PEAKS

BY MARCIA WILLIS

Executive Coordinators: Beppie Harrison
                        John Mason
Design Director: Guenther Radtke
Editorial: Isobel Campbell
           Damian Grint
           Marjorie Dickens
Picture Editor: Peter Cook
Research: Lynette Trotter
Cartography by Geographical Projects

This edition specially produced in 1973
for International Learning Systems
Corporation Limited, London
by Aldus Books Limited, London.

© 1971 Aldus Books Limited, London.

Printed and bound in Yugoslavia by
Mladinska Knjiga, Ljubljana

Contents

Left: two European explorers at the foot of a waterfall in the heart of South America. Even today, almost half of South America is a vast wilderness made up of high mountains, empty plains, and tropical jungles.

Frontispiece: H.M.S. *Beagle,* the ship in which the British naturalist Charles Darwin visited and explored South America in the years 1831–1835. In this painting the *Beagle* is seen at anchor in a bay off Tierra del Fuego.

List of Maps

The illuminated globe highlights in
blue the vast continent of South
America, the exploration of which is
the subject of this book. It describes
the adventures of men who traced the
rivers and climbed the mountain peaks
of South America, from the Portuguese
explorer Cabral who stumbled upon
Brazil by accident in 1500, to Percy
Fawcett, who disappeared without
trace in the Mato Grosso in 1925.

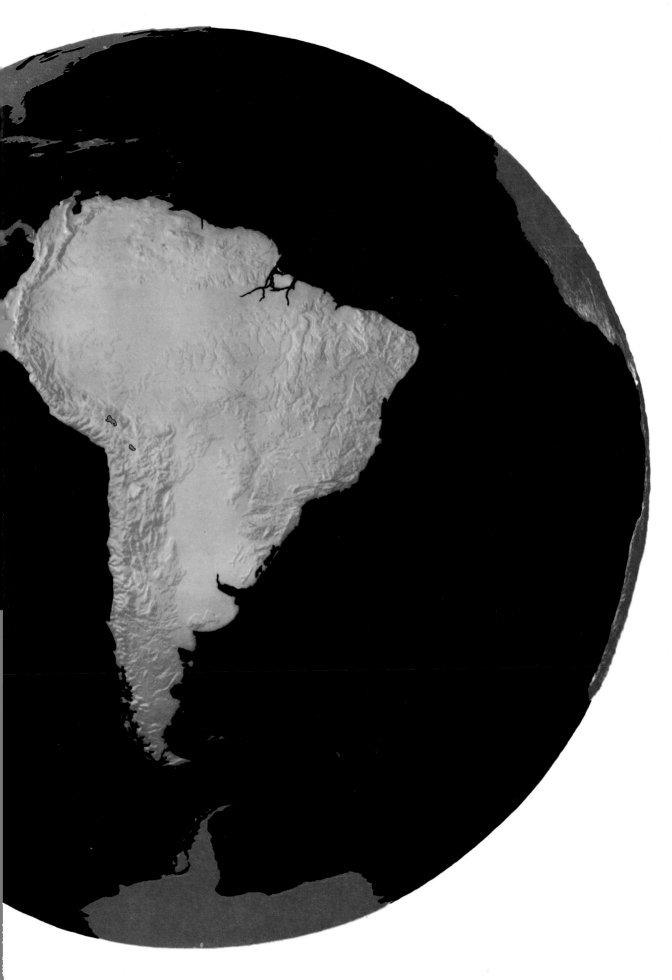

A Continent Discovered

1

To the first European explorer who sailed along its eastern coast, South America was a profound disappointment. No spice-laden cargo ships lined its shore. There were no bustling seaports. In fact, there was no sign of human life at all. All the explorer could see was an unbroken line of lush green jungle shimmering in the heat and apparently stretching for hundreds of miles.

The explorer, a Portuguese fleet commander named Pedro Álvares Cabral, was distressed by the view. Months before, his ship had been blown off course on its way down the West African coast while bound for India. Since then, Cabral had hoped that chance was taking him toward the long-sought western route to India. But the untamed land he saw before him showed no promise of yielding any kind of Eastern riches. And the hot, damp climate seemed to offer little respite from the hard voyage.

However, even this unwelcoming land was better than no land at all. The meager amount of food that was left on board was stale or wormeaten. The drinking water had gone foul. Cockroaches swarmed across the narrow decks. Rats scurried boldly out of the holds and through the cramped cabins. To the tired, hungry, increasingly rebellious crew, the new land looked like paradise.

So, on April 22, in the year 1500, Cabral dropped anchor and went ashore to raise the Portuguese flag over the land now known as Brazil. Although he did not know it, he was the first European to set foot on the South American continent. Eight years before,

Left: sturdy Spanish caravels, their sails swelling before the wind – a reconstruction in watercolors of the type of ship in the expedition that the Portuguese commander Pedro Álvares Cabral was leading to India. Blown off course by winds near the West African coast, the ships inadvertently crossed the Atlantic and made the first recorded discovery of the eastern coast of South America.

Right: Cabral, who had no idea that he had discovered a vast continent. As was customary with any new territory found, he claimed it for his king, but then set sail again for India as soon as his men had collected new supplies.

9

Christopher Columbus had discovered the West Indies, where there were already a number of thriving Spanish settlements. The Italian-born navigators John and Sebastian Cabot had cruised the North American shoreline in the service of England in 1497. But no one had even suspected the existence of a great southern continent.

We now know that the huge South American continent curves down into the Southern Hemisphere from a narrow land bridge that provides its only link with the north. Its spine, the Andes mountain range, is pressed against the Pacific Ocean. The continent faces Africa across the Atlantic Ocean.

Bordered on the north by the sunny Caribbean Sea and on the south by the stormy Antarctic, South America is a land of many contrasts. Its boundaries encircle jungles and highlands, deserts and rain forests, plains and rugged mountains, grassy plateaus and glaciers. All of these possess great regional diversity. The Brazilian

Above: one of the landings Amerigo Vespucci made along the coast of South America. Although he was impressed in general with the peacefulness of the people, this particular landing was more eventful—the boat was attacked by a force of men and women wearing war paint and feathers. The Portuguese overwhelmed them, and returned to their boat with 20 captives.

Right: South America, showing the main geophysical features, and the cities and political frontiers as they are today. The map emphasizes the extremes of climate and terrain that faced the explorers. The equator crosses South America near its widest point, and more than three-quarters of the continent lies in the tropics. But the southern tip is only about 600 miles from Antarctica.

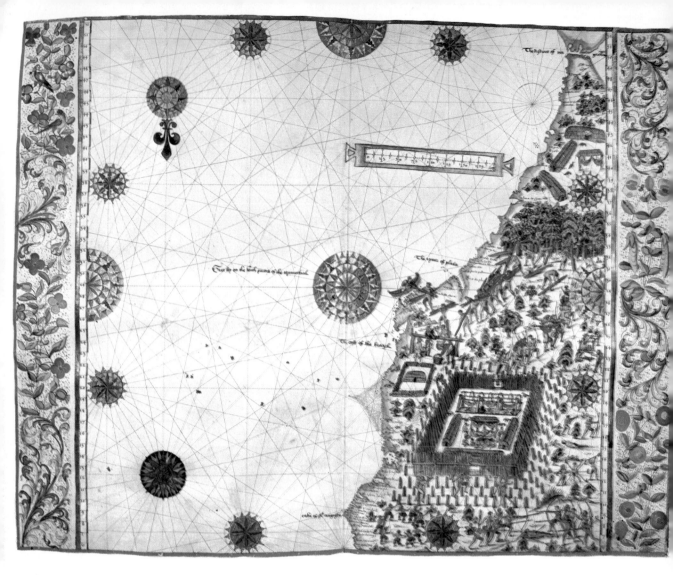

Above: a map of the 1700's showing the coast of Brazil, with many scenes of life in the new territory—Indians bartering wood from the jungle with the Portuguese, a group of Europeans going on a hunting party, a native village, and Indians fighting.
This map shows south at the top and north at the bottom.

jungles bear little resemblance to the jungles of Ecuador. The savannas of the north have different grasses, trees, and wildlife from the dusty pampa of the Gran Chaco, the great low-lying plain in Argentina that has the continent's hottest weather. The arid, desolate plains of Patagonia are different again. The Venezuelan Andes Mountains change character when they reach Chile. The rain forests of central South America change at each rise in elevation.

For millions of years, South America was an island continent. The isolation of the far-distant past is reflected in the vegetation and wildlife found there and nowhere else today. South America's unique plants and animals have had to adapt to a climate with a temperature range of over 100°F. They have had to be able to survive the rigors of a landscape that soars from sea level to a height of more than $3\frac{1}{2}$ miles.

South America has the world's longest and second-highest mountain chain. It has the widest area of continuous rain forest. And it has the river with the largest volume of water. South America has an abundance of metals, gems, spices, and exotic woods.

Right: an Aztec temple with a priest offering a human heart as a sacrifice to Huitzilopochtli, the god of the sun and of war. By the time Cortes arrived in Mexico the Aztec religion had become obsessed with human sacrifice. The reappearance of the peaceful white god, Quetzalcoatl, had been predicted for the very year in which Cortes and his men arrived, and Montezuma, the Aztec ruler, therefore treated the white invaders with awe and caution.

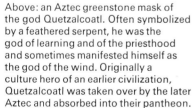

Above: an Aztec greenstone mask of the god Quetzalcoatl. Often symbolized by a feathered serpent, he was the god of learning and of the priesthood and sometimes manifested himself as the god of the wind. Originally a culture hero of an earlier civilization, Quetzalcoatl was taken over by the later Aztec and absorbed into their pantheon.

It boasts some of the world's richest soil and best grazing land.

Cabral, of course, had no inkling of the vastness of the land he had discovered. Apparently thinking that the soil he had stood on was part of an extension of the island chain Columbus had charted farther north, Cabral set sail for India as soon as possible.

During the late 1400's and early 1500's, Amerigo Vespucci, the Italian merchant explorer, made several expeditions to the north-eastern coast of Brazil. He, too, concluded that the land was part of Columbus' island chain. It was not until Vespucci's third and fourth voyages had taken him along the coasts of what are now Brazil, Uruguay, and Argentina in 1501–1502, that he was able to decide finally that this was not a part of Asia. The country that he discovered came to be called the New World.

"The land is very pleasant and full of an infinity of trees," Vespucci wrote. "At times the sweet scent of the grass and flowers and the taste of those fruits and roots is so wondrous that I could think myself close to paradise on earth ... who could count the woodland animals, such an abundance of tigers ... and other felines . . . and we saw so many other animals that I think so many kinds would be able to enter Noah's Ark only with difficulty."

Vespucci described the native peoples of this New World as having "no law or creed . . . they live in harmony with nature . . . they are well set up in body and well-proportioned, white in color, with a scanty beard or none." His account helped to foster the romantic idea of the *Noble Savage* that was later to become current in Europe.

News of Cabral's new "island" soon reached Portugal, and the Portuguese began to establish their first settlements in Brazil. Meanwhile, the Spaniards began to move south from their bases in the Caribbean Islands to colonize Central America. In 1509, they occupied Panama and established settlements all along its coast. A decade later, settlers began to raid the civilized Indian kingdoms to the north.

The Spaniards were ruthless conquerors. Spain, in the 1500's, was a corrupt, intolerant country with a rigid social caste system. The majority of the people were peasants living in poverty under the rule of a top-heavy upper class. The upper class consisted of clergy—Spain was an intensely religious country—*grandees* (great nobles), and lesser nobles called *hidalgos* and *caballeros*. Spain also had a tiny middle class of Jews and Moors, mostly tradesmen. In the 1500's, most of the middle class was driven out by the trials of the Spanish Inquisition. The Inquisition had been established by the Roman Catholic Church in order to seek out and punish all heretics—those persons who opposed orthodox church teachings.

Most hidalgos and caballeros were poor and illiterate. Many had nothing to boast of except a worthless title, but all shared an aristocratic contempt for manual labor. Military service in the colonies offered such men their only chance to win riches, status, and adventure. As soldiers, they brought to the New World the religious zeal of their homeland—and the intolerance that had given rise to the terrors of the Inquisition.

The Spaniards looked upon the pagan native inhabitants of the

text in image: tes é S. Juã d Vlua...

Above: envoys of the Aztec emperor Montezuma presenting gifts to Cortes. The ruler's messengers came to the coast where Cortes and his men had landed, with orders to treat the newcomers with respect but to report on their actions.

Left: an early manuscript illustration showing Cortes in combat with hostile Indian forces. Although the Spaniards were able to gain some Indian allies, the Aztec warriors fought bitterly against the invasion of their empire.

New World as creatures less than human. They slaughtered the Indians as if they were animals. The task was not difficult. The heavily armored Spanish soldiers attacked from horseback, which gave them an immediate tactical advantage. And native bows and arrows were almost useless against the invaders' muskets, swords, and cannon.

Moreover, the invaders had a silent ally—disease. Epidemics of smallpox and other alien diseases brought in by the Spaniards killed thousands of South American Indians during the invasions. Others were taken captive and enslaved. Most of these later died from malnutrition and exhaustion aboard the slaving ships.

The first native culture to fall before the Spanish invaders, known as *conquistadors* (conquerors), was the Aztec empire. The Aztec were originally a wandering tribe that migrated from the interior of

South America to create a kingdom in the swamps of Mexico.

Tenochtitlán, on the site of modern Mexico City, was the Aztec capital. It was built in the center of Lake Texcoco and connected to the shore by three wide earthen causeways (roads). These led out from the town like spokes from the hub of a wheel. They were linked to the land by movable drawbridges.

The Aztec were highly skilled craftsmen, architects, and farmers. They had a fair knowledge of astronomy and an accurate calendar. But although their culture had reached a high level of sophistication, it was slowly killing itself from within as the result of a repressive religion centered on human sacrifice. Each year, tens of thousands of captured warriors and members of subject states were sacrificed to the sun god, Huitzilopochtli. Streams of captives would be led to the tops of the temple-pyramids where they would have their hearts torn out to appease their insatiable god.

In November, 1521, a hidalgo named Hernando Cortes marched into Tenochtitlán with a force of about 1,000 men. They occupied the beautiful halls of the Aztec emperor, Montezuma II.

The emperor had made it easy for them. One of the beliefs of the Aztec religion was that the fair-skinned god of learning and of the priesthood, Quetzalcoatl, who had been driven away by his rival, Huitzilopochtli, would one day return home in triumph. Hearing of the advance of the Spanish invaders, Montezuma convinced himself that these were Quetzalcoatl and his allies. He ordered his subjects to let down the drawbridges for the returning god. Then he allowed himself to be taken prisoner in his own royal palace.

News of the gold and jewels that Cortes took from the Aztec quickly found its way back to Europe. Word spread rapidly of the boundless riches to be found in the New World. By the end of the 1500's, the French and English were vying for a share of the spoils. In the early 1700's, the Dutch also attempted to gain a foothold on the continent.

Cortes' victory over the Aztec was quickly followed by the Spanish conquest of the empire of the Maya on the Yucatán Peninsula. The Maya empire had long passed its peak, and was now on the wane. The Maya, however, were far more moderate in their religious beliefs than their Aztec neighbors to the northwest. In 1523, Pedro de Alvarado, one of Cortes' lieutenants, marched into Guatemala and conquered the Maya empire. But it was 1545 before the last of the Maya in the Yucatán surrendered to the conquistador Francisco de Montejo and his son.

But the biggest prize of all for the treasure-seekers lay farther to the south. This was the Inca empire, the largest Indian territory in South America. The ancestors of the Inca had lived in Peru from about 2000 B.C. In the 1500's, their empire occupied a strip of land that ran south from the Colombia-Ecuador border to central Chile, and from the Pacific Ocean to the eastern slopes of the Andes. It was the most advanced of the ancient Indian civilizations.

The Inca were highly organized socially. A rigid class system and

Left: a Mayan relief sculpture of about A.D. 700, a detail of a relief found running around the lintel of a Maya house. It shows a man who is mutilating his tongue by passing a cord set with thorns through it.

Below: Pizarro taking the Inca emperor Atahualpa prisoner. Pizarro's defeat of the emperor was callous. Taking advantage of Inca trust in a promise given, he assured Atahualpa of safety, but when the emperor came he was captured.

a strict government extended from the emperor and his council of four viceroys down to local officials in charge of units of only 10 families. While allowing little individual freedom, the system was very efficient. Under the direction of the government overseers, each family was responsible for farming its own tract of land as well as land owned by the priesthood and the government. Families also tended herds of alpaca and llama and worked in the emerald and gold mines.

The system had worked well for more than 400 years. But in the

early 1500's, as the Spaniards were discovering the New World, the Inca were facing their first serious internal crisis. The previous Inca ruler, Huayna Capac, had broken the age-old rules of succession to the throne. Against custom, he divided his empire into two parts in order to leave four-fifths to his legitimate heir, Huáscar, and the remaining northern section to Atahualpa, his son by a Quito princess. So when the Spaniards turned their armies south toward the Andes after their victories over the Aztec and the Maya they found the Inca empire torn by civil war.

The two men who conquered this richest and most civilized of the South American empires were illiterate, gold-hungry professional soldiers. They were caballeros who had come to the New World more than a decade before to make their fortunes. Both in their late 40's when they left Panama, they were older than the other conquistadors. Their names—Francisco Pizarro and Diego de Almagro—are synonymous with the most ruthless deeds of the invaders.

Pizarro was a cattle rancher in Panama, Almagro was a wandering adventurer. Intrigued by tales of the rich Inca empire, they decided to set out to find it. Their first attempt was in 1524, but they did not reach Peru. Their second attempt, in 1526, failed when heat and disease overcame the majority of the men. Pizarro was able to persuade only 13 men to go on with him. The rest returned to Panama. Then Almagro brought reinforcements and the combined group set out again. They reached a Peruvian port before returning to Panama.

In Panama, Pizarro and Almagro made up their minds that Pizarro should go to Spain to try to obtain the Spanish king's permission for the conquest of Peru. Permission was granted, funds were raised, and in 1531, Pizarro sailed again from Panama. He took with him his 3 brothers and about 180 men.

By the time Pizarro reached the city of Cajamarca in Peru, Atahualpa had already defeated Huáscar. Now only Atahualpa stood between the Spaniards and the treasure-filled Inca cities.

Determined to defeat the emperor as quickly as possible, Pizarro settled on a sure weapon—treachery. To the Inca, a man's word was a sacred bond. When Pizarro promised the emperor safe conduct if he came to Cajamarca for a parley, Atahualpa immediately accepted. Once he was inside the city, however, Pizarro and his men seized Atahualpa and slaughtered his attendants. The emperor, in a bid for freedom, offered a fortune in gold and silver to the Spaniards. He promised to fill a room 22 feet long by 17 feet wide with treasure in exchange for his freedom.

Pizarro agreed. In two months a stream of porters had finished filling the room with precious utensils, ornaments, and valuable religious objects gathered from all over the empire. But Atahualpa's reward for trusting Pizarro's word was death. Pizarro, reluctant to allow his powerful prisoner the freedom to rally his armies, had Atahualpa tried according to Spanish law, and executed.

Right: a Peruvian ceremonial knife, made during the 1300's or 1400's. It is gold decorated with turquoise. Precious objects like this were brought from all over the empire to fill the ransom room at Cajamarca in Atahualpa's desperate bid for his freedom. But Pizarro did not keep his part of the bargain, and the hapless Inca emperor was eventually tried according to Spanish law and executed.

Above: faced with the wretchedness and horror of life under Spanish domination many of the Indians, as shown in this picture, chose to kill themselves and their children rather than exist under the soul-destroying conditions of degradation and servitude. It is difficult to imagine what it must have been like to have the whole pattern of civilization crumble within the lifespan of a single generation. Villages that had existed for centuries were decimated, and the few survivors enslaved.

With the emperor dead, the land of the Inca was in turmoil. Pizarro easily crushed what remained of any organized resistance. He advanced to the Inca capital, and put a puppet-ruler, a relative of Huáscar, on the throne.

One other Indian kingdom still remained. On a Colombian plateau in the upper Andes, lived the Chibcha Indians who were divided into two warring states, ruled by two tyrannical chiefs. Though less powerful than the other great empires, the Chibcha were nonetheless accomplished builders of stone temples, highways, and bridges as well as farmers and traders. They mined emeralds and salt, which they exchanged with other tribesmen for wood, skins, and cacao seeds (from which cocoa is made). Their temples were filled with gold and silver carvings, often studded with gems.

In 1536, a contingent of 166 soldiers, led by a young Spanish ex-lawyer named Gonzalo Jiménez de Quesada, set out on a nine-month march across the steaming Magdalena River Valley toward the Chibcha kingdom. The men struggled through insect-infested swamps that were a haven for giant alligators, jaguars, and deadly snakes. But the ordeal was worth it. After slaughtering and torturing hundreds of the passive Chibcha Indians, Quesada and his men emerged with close to a million dollars' worth of booty.

There were still some less civilized tribes that would take longer to subdue. For example, the warlike Araucanian Indians of Chile, often called "the Apache of South America," continued to attack Spanish settlers until the end of the 1800's. And there were dozens of other small nomadic tribes, some of which continued to harass the Spaniards both on the pampas and on the Patagonian plains for several hundred years.

By about 1525, the Spaniards had surveyed the whole of South America's eastern coastline. By the 1550's, they had explored and mapped the entire western coastline. And by the end of the 1500's, the great Indian civilizations had been all but wiped out. The majority had been conquered in the first 25 years. With a handful of men, the Spaniards had subdued some 20 million South American Indians. An estimated 12 million were enslaved as feudal serfs, living in the towns and villages springing up across the country. The rest—some 8 million—had died, either in battle, from disease, from hard labor, or from the sorrow that comes from hopelessness. The innocent people Amerigo Vespucci had described so lyrically were no longer free.

Right: the death of the Inca emperor. After Pizarro had tricked and executed Atahualpa, his leaderless people were in turmoil. It was then relatively easy for the Spaniards to crush what remained of his once-splendid empire.

E ME STA TA/OA ESTA
ba prouimsia das Amazonasa com ho seu grande
Rio besta a prouimsia dos vragas ho novo Reinoo
ha margarita ho Reino deborbunta ho peru as anti
lhas a fera firme as fomduras as charcas ho Reino
de mexico a nova espanha ho mar do sul ho Reino
de quatimala a ilha de cuba ha de Iamaica ha Ilha
espanhola a ilha de porto Rigo o golfo de valemsue
lla ho Rio grande a prouimsia dos topaios

Mar Do Sul

Operu

Iago

cariba

Rio das amazonas

Guatimala

Iamaica

Antilhas

Puerto rico

Espan

Orellana Explores the Amazon

2

Above: Francisco de Orellana, one of the Spanish conquistadors who went with Gonzalo Pizarro from Ecuador to find the fabled land of El Dorado. What he found instead was the great Amazon River, which he and his men followed all the way to the Atlantic. Left: a map of the New World drawn in 1563 by Luis Lazaro. It shows a vast river—the Amazon—snaking its way across the continent. In this map West is at the top.

During the first decades of European conquest and settlement, the Spaniards and Portuguese pieced together only small fragments of the huge map of South America. So little was known about it that groups of men could set off in almost any direction knowing they would find new, entirely unexplored regions. Hints from early travelers and local Indians of wealth and prized natural resources sent explorers off on many unmapped journeys. Adventurers braved great stretches of virgin territory in their search for undiscovered tribes and the fabulous riches they were rumored to possess. Geographical discovery was never the only motive for their travels, but often it was the only result. Gradually, the great physical features of the continent began to be put on the map.

The mightiest river in the world begins modestly in the foothills of the towering Peruvian Andes Mountains. There, two of its smaller tributaries, the Marañón and the Ucayali, join together. Near these headwaters, early in 1541, a Spaniard named Francisco de Orellana set sail on a third tributary, the Napo, on a voyage into history.

At its source, the giant river is deceptively small, surpassed in depth and breadth by at least a dozen other South American rivers. But as it flows eastward across the Brazilian border, the belly of the stream begins to swell. At midpoint it is more than 10 miles wide and 350 feet deep.

As it follows its lazy path across the continent to the sea, the river is fed by more than 200 jungle tributaries. When it finally reaches the Atlantic, its 90-mile-wide mouth disgorges more water than the Nile, Mississippi, and Yangtze rivers combined.

The only force equal to the huge river is the Atlantic itself. Twice daily great ocean tides sweep in across the delta. A 15-foot wall of salt water rolls up the river, penetrating 600 miles upstream. In turn the river sends its muddy currents 200 miles into the sea on the ebb tide.

This is the Amazon, 3,900 miles long from its source to the sea. Even with all the resources of modern equipment, very few men have traveled safely the whole length of the river. But the Spaniard Orellana did it, although that was not his aim when he set off down the Napo River.

Orellana's story starts with his march to Quito, the capital of Ecuador, in March, 1540. His intention was to join Gonzalo Pizarro on a brief expedition to find wealth for the Spanish throne. He had no idea that during 1541 he would travel right across South America, from the Andes Mountains to the Atlantic Ocean, would fight dozens of battles with hostile tribes, and nearly die of starvation in the course of his struggle to reach the sea.

Gonzalo Pizarro was as ruthless and gold-hungry as his older brother Francisco, the conquistador. Francisco sent Gonzalo to South America to search for treasure. He was to attempt to find the kingdom that legend said was richest of all—that of El Dorado, the gilded king, who was supposed to anoint himself daily with gold dust. Gonzalo hoped, too, to reach the fabled Lands of Cinnamon. Cinnamon was in great demand among Europeans as a pleasant flavoring to improve the taste of their often not very fresh food. The spice was found only in tropical regions, and in the 1500's was worth nearly its weight in gold to Europeans.

Gonzalo Pizarro arrived in Ecuador at a time when Orellana was becoming bored with his job as lieutenant governor of two small Ecuadorian cities. Orellana had already distinguished himself as a soldier in fights against the Inca and in the conquest of Cusco and Lima. He was an adventurer, not a bureaucrat. The young nobleman lost no time in volunteering his services to an expedition that promised adventure. Pizarro was impressed by Orellana's offer to enlist the help of friends and to donate money to the expedition. He invited the younger man to join the expedition at once.

Moving south from Ecuador along the little Cocoa River, Pizarro's army of 4,000 Indians and about 300 Spaniards must have been a formidable sight. To feed them all, he took along

Above: a Peruvian girl herding llama. The Spanish were quick to use these curious animals to carry their supplies, as Gonzalo Pizarro did on the march from Ecuador to the Napo River Valley.

several thousand live hogs, squealing, snorting, and constantly charging their Indian herders in an attempt to escape. There were hundreds of llamas to carry supplies and provide meat in an emergency. There were dozens of horses. There were more than 2,000 bloodhounds. These were to be used not only to hunt game but also to subdue the local Indians.

Pizarro met early disappointment. Taking a small party of men on ahead to spy out the territory, he had to return $2\frac{1}{2}$ months later with the news that there were no riches at all to be found in the area.

He had seen a few precious cinnamon trees, but they were widely

Left: the Spanish siege of the Inca city of Cusco, one of the battles in which they established their rule over the empire of Atahualpa. Orellana was one of the young adventurers who proved his competence in this battle. Right: a llama pack train, heavily laden with supplies, overseen by a European and his Indian slaves in the mountains of South America. Many such convoys must have traveled along the narrow trails in the years when the explorers searched feverishly for the cities of gold and glory.

scattered through the valley. The local Indians had been unable to guide him toward more fertile lands or the fabled treasures. They knew of no El Dorado and no Lands of Cinnamon. Beyond the valley of the Napo River, they said, lay only the jungle. And cutting through the vast wilderness to the south was a giant river.

Gonzalo Pizarro was not interested in rivers. He wanted wealth for the Spanish throne and for the renown it would bring him. Enraged by what the Indians told him, he ordered his men to burn some of them alive. Others he had torn to pieces by his dogs.

News of the murders traveled fast in the valley. Afterward the Indians seldom told the Spaniards the truth. Learning that the Europeans preferred tall tales about fertile valleys and golden temples to dull fact, the Indians became accomplished story tellers. Their stories fed the Spaniards' lust for gold, and led the adventurers on into the treacherous *selvas*—the rain forests that extend from southern Venezuela into northern Brazil.

Above: Pizarro setting dogs on the Indians who refused to tell him where he could find gold. Convinced that incredible wealth was there for the taking, if only the Indians could be induced to show them the way, the Spaniards resorted to terrible cruelty. Not surprisingly, the Indians soon learned to tell tales of gold-laden cities, generally several days' march away from their own poor villages.

Above right: the Spanish building a boat. Pizarro ordered the building of a small brigantine—the *San Pedro*—in which Orellano could sail on down the river in search of food.

Right: in the ruthless intrigues of the established colonies, rife with plots and counterplots, death could be sudden. Gonzalo Pizarro, a victim of his own greed, was beheaded in 1548.

VERAGVA PARS.

By the time Pizarro returned to the main camp, the food was already almost gone. The pigs and llamas had all been eaten and the men were killing dogs for food. All but a few of the 4,000 Indians had died. Many had perished of cold and fatigue during the trek across the Andes Mountains. Many more died in the continuous tropical rain of the selvas.

The massive death toll left the Spaniards with no one to carry their food and arms—tasks they considered below the dignity of a soldier. So when they reached the banks of the Cocoa River, which flows into the Napo, Pizarro ordered the remaining men to stop and build a boat to carry the sick, and the heavy supplies. In less than a month, they had built a brigantine, a two-masted square-rigged ship, out of native hardwood. They called it the *San Pedro*.

But before the expedition could travel farther, the men had to find food. By now they were eating roots, nuts, and berries. They had flushed out all the game in the area long before. The Indian

27

guides informed them that there was abundant food only a day's journey away.

Near the junction of the Cocoa and Napo rivers, Pizarro ordered Orellana to take some of the men aboard the *San Pedro* and sail down the Napo in search of food. Promising to be back within two weeks, Orellana weighed anchor and sailed away. He did not return.

Months later, Pizarro's group, deprived now of the boat and supplies, managed to reach the junction of the "great rivers"— probably the Napo and its tributary, the Curaray. There they found signs that Orellana had been ashore and had left weeks before. Exhausted, and with their clothes rotting on their backs, Pizarro and his men had no alternative but to retrace their path to Quito.

"Paying no heed to what he owed to the services of your majesty," Pizarro wrote indignantly to the Spanish king, "[Orellana] went down the river . . . leaving only the signs and choppings showing how they had been on land and had stopped at the junction of the rivers. . . . He had thus displayed toward the whole expeditionary force the greatest cruelty that ever faithless men have shown."

It was 1542 before the survivors of Gonzalo Pizarro's expedition straggled into Quito, sick with fever and near starvation. Bitter about his failure to find gold and about the hardships he had suffered, Pizarro was convinced that Orellana had deliberately deceived him. In those days of court intrigues and rivalry, the claim could have been justified. But Orellana's explanation is equally likely. He contended that finding himself swept along by a fast current farther and farther from camp with no sight of the promised food, he had had no choice but to press on. Turning back through the barren countryside would have been suicidal.

Orellana was probably unable to read or write, as were most of the hidalgos who went with him. But a complete account of the

Above: the fabulous creatures of the river reported by the explorers. The men were faced, in a hostile and strange environment, with fish and animals they had never seen before. If they were not the monsters shown here, they were certainly often frightening to come upon unexpectedly.

Above and right: piranha fish, the fearsome flesh-eaters found in some South American waters. They remain a formidable hazard for present-day travelers. For Orellana and his party, drifting down an unknown river on which every bend might conceal rapids that would throw everyone into the muddy waters, the small fish flashing in ominous circles beneath them must have had a truly nightmarish quality. Armed with savage sharp teeth that can slash through stranded wire, they attack large animals. The Indians, familiar with their ways, have always treated them with guarded respect.

Above: the vast Amazon, although not the longest, certainly the greatest river in the world, tranquil at sunset. Orellana's expedition was the first to explore the river, although it had apparently been briefly entered from the sea by a party under the Spanish navigator Vincente Pinzón around 1500.

journey was kept by a Dominican friar called Gaspar de Carvajal. Scholars think that except for his versions of some of the stories the Indians told, the document is an accurate description of the adventures of the crew of the *San Pedro*.

Orellana found no food for more than 500 miles down the Napo. By that time, he and his 57 men were nearly dead from starvation. "We had reached a privation so great that we were eating nothing but leather, belts, and the soles of our shoes cooked with herbs," wrote Carvajal. "So great was our weakness that we could not remain standing, for some on all fours and others with staffs went to the woods for a few roots to eat. They were . . . like madmen and did not possess sense."

In a worse climate, Orellana's expedition would almost certainly have perished. But despite its closeness to the equator, the Amazon basin is not unbearably hot. Even in midsummer, which it then was, the temperature seldom climbs above 90°F.

Still, it must have been a terrifying voyage. Drifting down the frothing, muddy river, with the rain forests rising like green cliffs

from each bank, the crew of the *San Pedro* was totally isolated. Turning back was impossible. In their weakened state, the men could scarcely lift their oars to battle with the current.

Parrots screeched from the trees, and the eerie voices of howler monkeys echoed across the water. Huge *caymans,* reptiles closely resembling alligators, slid silently from the bank to drift in the boat's wake. Giant *capybara,* the largest rodents in the world, wallowed on the shore. In the murky water below, circled schools of the flesh-eating *piranha.* These little fish will attack animals much larger than themselves, and their sharp teeth can bite through double-stranded copper wire. The men's skins were soon swollen and discolored from the swarms of insects that descended on them in clouds. But the worst hardship was the mental one. The river ahead was entirely unknown. Around each bend might lie the threat of "white water"—rapids that would dash the boat against the rocks. Or there might be the brink of a waterfall that would carry them all to their death. On January 3, 1541, the *San Pedro*'s crew first heard the sound of drums and knew they were approaching an Indian settlement.

Despite the crew's physical weakness, their superior weapons easily overpowered the Indians' bows and arrows in this first encounter. Orellana could probably have slaughtered all the inhabitants. But his instincts were not as cruel as were Pizarro's. He managed to communicate with the Indians in their own language. He assured them of his peaceful intentions, and the Indians introduced him to the overlords of a dozen neighboring tribes. They promised him food and a peaceful passage through their territories.

Early in February, 1541, Orellana reached the junction of the Napo and the Amazon. He was probably not the first white man to discover the river. Forty-one years before, an expedition led by

Right: Vincente Pinzón, who discovered the mouth of the Amazon, seen here with his men in combat with another vessel. Like many of the adventurers of the period, Pinzón was quick to seek riches wherever they might be found, and occasionally, piracy seemed as profitable as exploration. These pitched battles between ships must have been common occurrences.

the Spanish navigator Vincente Pinzón is believed to have entered its mouth and traveled 50 miles upstream. Pinzón named the river Rio Santa Maria de la Mar Dulce—the River Saint Mary of the Sweet Sea. Orellana, however, was unquestionably the first man to explore the Amazon. In the process he became the first European to cross the South American continent.

As the boat approached the Amazon from the Napo, the width of the main river astonished Orellana. Apparently, he concluded that the expedition was nearing the river's mouth. His thoughts turned to the hazards of ocean travel, and he began preparations for building a larger boat.

"With the boat we were using, if God saw fit to guide us to the sea, we could not go on out to a place of rescue," wrote Carvajal, "for this reason it was necessary to apply our wits to building another brigantine of greater burden."

The building of the *San Pedro* had been a remarkable feat. It was even more remarkable that a few dozen soldiers with no knowledge of shipbuilding could undertake construction of a larger boat deep in the jungle. Carvajal describes how the men dug pits and made buckskin bellows to fan the flames of the charcoal fire, where they forged "2,000 very good nails." Then they cut planks out of local hardwoods. All in all, it took two months to build the second boat, the *Victoria*.

Whenever they reached a friendly settlement, the crew were able to stock up with food—turtles, tapirs, game birds, and fish. They salted and preserved as much as they could. But on long stretches of the river they had to endure days without any food at all.

By mid-May, the *San Pedro* and the *Victoria* were well down the Amazon and approaching the junction with the Juruá River. This region was ruled by the Indian overlord Machipora. Until now, the Spaniards had enjoyed friendly treatment from local tribes. From this point on they were not so lucky.

"We saw coming up the river a great many canoes, all equipped for fighting, gaily colored and with . . . shields . . . made out of the shell-like skins of lizards and the hides of manatees and of tapirs as tall as a man," wrote the friar, "they were coming on with great yell, playing on many drums and wooden trumpets, threatening us as if they were going to devour us."

Drawing the brigantines together to create a solid front, the Spaniards finally succeeded in pushing back the Indians and gaining a foothold on shore. But as a Spanish raiding party returned from the village with food, the Indians attacked again in force. "There were more than 2,000 Indians," Carvajal writes, "of the companions [the Spaniards] . . . there were only ten, and they had much to do to defend themselves."

Other Spaniards rushed to help. They emerged from their first major battle with 18 men wounded, 6 badly, "some being pierced through the arms and others through the legs." One man died in the assault.

Above: a tapir browses on the banks of the Amazon River today. As the *Victoria* and the *San Pedro* drifted down the mighty river, they stocked up on food whenever they reached a settlement. There they would salt and preserve as much meat as possible— that of turtles, tapirs, and anything else available—against future famine.

Right: the capture of an Indian village, from an early manuscript. Orellana's policy of dealing more humanely than Pizarro with the Indians had won his expedition local friendship. But when they reached the junction of the Amazon with the Juruá River they were faced with fierce hostility. They went 1,000 miles before they were able to capture a village and reprovision the ships.

Faced with such overwhelming numbers of Indians, Orellana ordered his men to load aboard what food they could. As soon as possible they pushed on down the river, pursued by hundreds of war canoes.

When they finally captured an Indian village, the crew had traveled almost 1,000 miles nonstop since leaving the Napo. The exhausted men celebrated by staying there for three days "resting, regaling ourselves with good lodging, eating all we wanted."

As they traveled farther, Orellana was able to see from the deck large stone-built highways cutting through the jungle "like royal highways and wider." Were these the fabled highways of the Inca? Orellana had no chance to find out. Between the junction of the Juruá and the sea, the Amazon's shores were ever more thickly settled with increasingly hostile tribes. After he had ventured a few miles inland on one of the roads, Orellana's fear of ambush drove him back to the ship. "He saw it was not prudent to go on . . . and said to the companions that it would be well to depart at once."

Carvajal tells that on one occasion the Spaniards stopped at a great villa on the river bank. It contained a hoard of fine pottery.

The workmanship bore witness to the skill of the Inca as artists and craftsmen. "[The pottery was] made of porcelain of the best that has ever been seen in the world . . . that of Málaga [world famous for its beautiful ornaments] is not its equal . . . it is all glazed and embellished with colors so bright that they astonish. More than this, the drawings and paintings on them . . . are . . . accurately worked out."

On June 3, the *Victoria* and *San Pedro* were tossed about in the currents of the huge Negro River. The Negro River is the Amazon's widest tributary, flowing 1,400 miles southeast from Colombia to join the main river. Carvajal describes its water as "as black as ink"— a result of the black mud the Negro River carries. Farther on, the ships passed a river junction where "the Indians . . . rose up more than 5,000 strong, armed, and they began to shoot at us and challenge us."

A few days later, the travelers awoke to a grisly sight. On the south shore, relates Carvajal, "there were seven gibbets [gallows] . . . and on the gibbets were nailed many dead men's heads." This was the territory of a tribe of head hunters. The friar named it the Province of the Gibbets.

Although they were well aware of the hazards of landing on this stretch of river, the Spaniards were forced to go ashore for food. For several weeks, they managed to escape a confrontation with the Indians. Then, on June 24, the ships rounded a bend in the river and drifted into a battle that would later become famous throughout the civilized world: Orellana's fight with the "Amazon women." The battle caught the imagination of Europe. Ironically, the river was finally named after the warrior women instead of after Orellana. In the public's eagerness to hear more about the warriors, who so closely resembled the mythical maidens of Greek and Roman legend, Orellana's discovery was largely overlooked.

The Amazons were said to live far in the interior in great houses. They ate off golden plates and wore necklaces and bracelets of gold, studded with precious gems. According to one legend, the Amazons would receive warriors from a neighboring tribe for a few days once a year. The female children born of this union would be raised by the Amazons while the males were either returned to their fathers the following year, or killed at birth.

"We ourselves saw [them] fighting in front of all the Indian men . . ." claimed Carvajal, "and [they] fought so courageously that the Indian men did not dare to turn their backs. . . . These women are very white and tall and have hair very long and braided and wound about the head, and they are very robust and go about naked but with their privy parts covered."

Carvajal probably did see women fighting, but he may well have embroidered his description of them with tales the Indians told him. Most historians doubt that there really was a tribe of Amazons. They point out that it was not uncommon for Indian women to fight alongside their men. The men themselves wore their hair very long

Above: a map of the 1400's by Le Testu, showing the barbarous habits of the Indians of Brazil, chopping limbs off their prisoners and cooking them over fires. In fact, there was little to choose between the brutal methods of the conquistadors and the traditional savagery of many Amazon Indian tribes.

Left: a head shrunken by the Jivaro Indian tribe. Carvajal reported his sighting of the trophies of a tribe of head-hunters. The heads were shrunk by a long, slow process of heating.

and could, therefore, easily have been mistaken for women.

After fighting for hours, the Spaniards managed to get away. The battle had left the two ships studded with arrows, like the quills on a porcupine.

Drifting on, Orellana's ships had almost reached the mouth of the Amazon when they ran into another Indian ambush. In the fighting that followed, several men were fatally wounded. Carvajal was blinded in one eye by an arrow. However, despite excruciating pain, he managed to continue his daily journal.

The going was more hazardous now. Floating driftwood, washed in on the tide, dashed against the boats and damaged them. Several times Orellana was forced to beach the boats for repairs. But the delta islands proved to be dangerous havens. They were inhabited

by cannibals who used poison arrows. The tip of each arrow was smeared with the deadly poison called *curare*. Curare is a thick black syrup made from poisonous plants. When injected into the blood stream or outer tissues of man and other mammals it paralyzes the muscles. The victim usually dies of suffocation when the breathing muscles are affected. After one of the crew was killed by a poison-tipped arrow, the men collected all the food they could carry so that they would not have to go ashore again.

"When we saw . . . the poison, we proposed not to put foot on land in a settled district unless . . . from sheer necessity," wrote Carvajal. Despite their caution, another crew member was killed, scratched by an arrow fired from shore, before the boats reached the sea.

The friar was amazed by the size of the mouth of the Amazon. ". . . The whole, as we saw farther back, from point to point, must be over 50 leagues [between three and four miles]. It sends out into the sea fresh water for more than 25 leagues; it rises and falls 6 or 7 fathoms."

Safe now from Indian attacks, Orellana still had to fight the *bores,* (great tidal waves) that rush in from the Atlantic, raising the level of the river as much as 15 feet. Buffeted by waves and drifting timber, the *Victoria* slowly made its way out to sea. But as they were setting their course for one of the Spanish Caribbean islands, the crew of the *Victoria* lost sight of its tiny sister ship. After hours of searching, they concluded sadly that the *San Pedro* was lost.

The *Victoria* sailed on up the coast alone, almost sinking off the coast of Trinidad. Orellana had made a navigational error, and the ship drifted into the Gulf of Paria, a square bay almost completely enclosed between the island of Trinidad and the mainland of Venezuela. The Spaniards were trapped by the treacherous tides for a week. "We tried to go out to sea again," wrote Carvajal, "but

Left: a Greek frieze showing the famous, legendary Amazon women in the midst of battle with Greek soldiers. In the myth they were fierce warriors whose whole society was organized for their frequent wars with outsiders.

Right: a contemporary view of the women warriors of the Amazon River. It seems unlikely, however, that there was really a tribe of fighting women. In many tribes Indian women would fight with the men—who, with their long hair and, unlike the Europeans, beardless faces, might themselves be mistaken for women.

Below: the mouth of the Amazon River, opening on the Atlantic Ocean. The part of the voyage leading out into the ocean was one of the most perilous, with Orellana fighting tidal bores, heavy driftwood battering his ships, and attacks of local Indians armed with arrows tipped with deadly curare.

getting out was so difficult that it took us seven days . . . during all of which time our companions never dropped the oars from their hands. We came very close to staying inside there forever."

Two days after leaving the gulf, the *Victoria* finally sailed into the harbor of Nueva Cadiz on Cubagua. To the crew's delight they found that the *San Pedro* had arrived a few days before. During the time that they had thought it was lost, the smaller boat had been traveling parallel to the *Victoria*. For much of the voyage it had probably been little over a mile away.

A few weeks later Orellana and Carvajal sailed for Spain with the news of their amazing adventure. Europe found it too incredible to believe. Instead of acclaiming the two men as brave explorers, the public ridiculed them. Scholars accused them of inventing the whole story.

Carvajal shrugged off the hostile reception and returned to Peru.

Right: northern South America, showing the routes of the earliest European explorers. The map covers the period between the discovery of the continent by Pedro Cabral in 1500, to the tragic voyage of Sir Walter Raleigh in 1616-1617. The green highlights the areas that became known during this period.

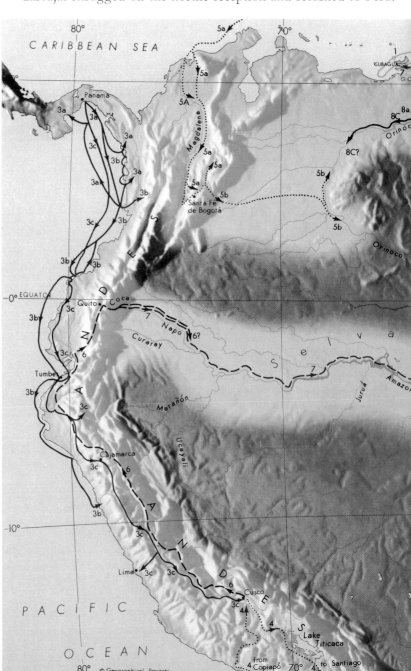

He rose in the hierarchy of the church and lived to be a very old man. Orellana determined to go back and explore the Amazon again, this time from its mouth, to bring home more evidence in support of his claims. In his haste to return, Orellana was careless in his preparations. The four boats he equipped for the voyage were riddled with dry rot. Two went down in the middle of the Atlantic. The others sank before they had crossed the delta. Under constant attack by Indians and suffering from recurrent fever, Orellana's crew mutinied. They refused to go any farther.

Exhausted by the voyage, weakened by disease, and disheartened by failure, Orellana gave up his quest. He had put the whole length of the Amazon on the map. Several explorers of different nationalities were to fill in sections of the vast Amazon basin. But in the next centuries only a tiny handful of men were to emulate Orellana's achievement in crossing the continent.

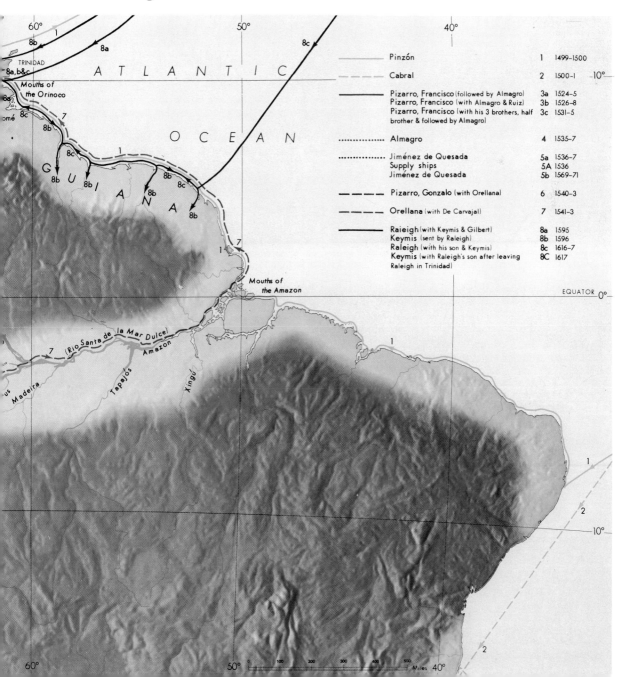

———— Pinzón	1	1499–1500
- - - - Cabral	2	1500–1
———— Pizarro, Francisco (followed by Almagro)	3a	1524–5
Pizarro, Francisco (with Almagro & Ruiz)	3b	1526–8
Pizarro, Francisco (with his 3 brothers, half brother & followed by Almagro)	3c	1531–5
·········· Almagro	4	1535–7
·········· Jiménez de Quesada	5a	1536–7
Supply ships	5A	1536
Jiménez de Quesada	5b	1569–71
— — — Pizarro, Gonzalo (with Orellana)	6	1540–3
— — — Orellana (with De Carvajal)	7	1541–3
———— Raleigh (with Keymis & Gilbert)	8a	1595
Keymis (sent by Raleigh)	8b	1596
Raleigh (with his son & Keymis)	8c	1616–7
Keymis (with Raleigh's son after leaving Raleigh in Trinidad)	8C	1617

The Search for El Dorado

3

Left: Sir Walter Raleigh with his son, also named Walter, painted in 1602. It was in an attempt to regain favor at court that he set out to find the fabulous city of gold in the jungle.

Below: Manoa, the city of El Dorado, from a German book of 1599. The tale of Juan Martinez about the lost capital of the Inca captured the imagination of gold-hungry Europe.

MANOA odel DORADO.

In 1597, a Spaniard named Juan Martinez stumbled out of the jungles of Guiana, now Venezuela, half dead from fever. He raved about an incredible adventure to the soldiers he met. Martinez claimed that 10 years earlier, while on a Spanish military exploring expedition, he had been captured by a group of Indians. They had taken him to a fabulous city which he called Manoa. This, he said, was a lost capital of the Inca, the city of El Dorado, the golden kingdom.

Within the walls of the city, Martinez said, there were golden sidewalks, temples, and gardens filled with glittering ferns, flowers, and herbs, all delicately fashioned out of the precious metal. The Spaniard recounted how the king and his courtiers anointed themselves with oil and gold dust before holding court.

Martinez said that he had finally been freed by his captors and left blindfolded in the jungle. They had laden him with golden gifts. But, he claimed, he was later accosted by different, hostile Indians. They robbed him of all but a few trinkets. This explained why, when he returned to camp, he had little proof of his amazing adventure.

Was the story only the raving of a delirious man? Or was it proof at last that there really was a great kingdom of El Dorado? Throughout the 1500's, the legend of El Dorado had gained great currency among European soldiers and settlers. In the early decades numerous adventurers set off in search of the golden kingdom. They searched in vain the whole area between the coast of Venezuela and the banks of the Amazon. Many expeditions ended in tragedy. Some explorers were killed by hostile Indians. Others were lost forever in unknown territory. But the legend had persisted. Might Martinez' story be true?

The great English soldier and writer Sir Walter Raleigh had always been intrigued by the tale. Martinez' story gave him encouragement. He determined to search for the huge gold mine that was said to supply the capital. The mine was supposed to be located several hundred miles up the great Orinoco River. Raleigh made up his mind to claim it for England.

When Raleigh first set out for Guiana, he was a handsome, vigorous man of 43. He was at the height of his popularity with the public. Renowned for his military exploits, Raleigh was also celebrated for his wit, admired for his poetic talent, and respected for a mind that ranged easily from art, to philosophy, to science.

He had for years been a special favorite of Queen Elizabeth I. But his fortunes at court were on the decline. In 1594, he had secretly married the beautiful Elizabeth Throckmorton, one of the queen's ladies-in-waiting.

Elizabeth was furious when she heard of the secret wedding. Despite the fact that she had a new favorite at court, Elizabeth did not want any other woman to have Raleigh. She commanded that Raleigh and his new wife be thrown into the Tower of London. The confinement in the Tower was a harsh way of telling Raleigh that his days at court were over. Although not deprived of his estates and business enterprises, he would no longer be welcome on the queen's councils or in her salon.

When he was released after a few months' imprisonment, Raleigh found the absence from court intrigue unbearable. He listened, frustrated, as friends told him of the growing rivalry between the queen's current favorite, Lord Essex, and her adviser, the conniving William Cecil, Lord Burghley.

Determined to regain the queen's favor, Raleigh began to brood about the best way to achieve it. After weeks of thought, he decided upon a solution. He would undertake an expedition to Guiana in search of El Dorado. Raleigh reasoned that the idea would have a twofold appeal to the queen. A successful expedition would enrich England's treasury. It would also deal a humiliating blow to Spanish claims of sovereignty in northern South America. England and Spain were deadly enemies at the time. The English hated the Spaniards principally because they jealously guarded the rich fields that their exploration had opened up and refused to allow any other country to share in them.

Raleigh presented his plan to Elizabeth. Although her reactions were not particularly enthusiastic, the queen ordered him to proceed.

Raleigh left from Plymouth harbor on February 6, 1595, aboard a small three-masted sailing ship. Three other ships sailed with him. There was a total expeditionary force of 150 men. Included in the company were Raleigh's cousin, his nephew John Gilbert, and his

Left: Raleigh's attack on Trinidad in 1595. He organized the raid to show his disapproval of the cruelty of the Spanish toward the Indians, and also because he did not want the Spanish fleet to hinder his movements.

former classmate and friend from Oxford days Lawrence Keymis.

The little fleet landed in Trinidad. There the seamen awaited the arrival of some other ships that were to join the expedition. Raleigh organized a raid on the Spanish fleet occupying the harbor. The attack was partly a precautionary measure. Raleigh had no desire to be caught on the island with a vigorous Spanish fleet hemming him in. But he was also moved by Indian tales of Spanish cruelty and wanted to show his disapproval.

After a few weeks of fighting, Raleigh managed to capture the Spanish governor of Trinidad Antonio de Berrio. Berrio had had years of experience in remote Spanish outposts in South America. He had met and talked often with Juan Martinez. Berrio, like Raleigh, had a highly romantic imagination. He spoke repeatedly of his conviction that El Dorado did exist. But he tried to dissuade

Above: Elizabeth I in a ceremonial procession, in a painting attributed to Robert Peake the elder. Flattered lavishly by her courtiers, Elizabeth insisted on absolute loyalty. She considered that the secret marriage of her favorite, Raleigh, was a slight to her dignity as a woman and a queen.

43

Raleigh from going in search of it. Berrio said the distances to be traveled to the fabled mine were too great. His warnings only served to convince the Englishman of the existence of the golden kingdom.

The other ships arrived, and Raleigh and his crew left Trinidad to sail to the mouth of the Orinoco. Raleigh described the river in his book *Discovery of Guiana*. "The Great River of Orenoque or Barawuan has nine branches which fall out on the north side of his own main mouth. On the south side it has seven other fallings into the sea, so it disemboqueth [flows out] by sixteen arms in all, between islands and broken ground."

Raleigh was to become an expert on the "labyrinth of rivers" that was the mouth of the Orinoco. A few weeks after his arrival in Guiana, Raleigh's boats became hopelessly lost in the giant maze of the river's tributaries. He and his men had to capture an Indian canoe and use the captives as guides before they were able to find their way out.

"I know all the earth doth not yield the like confluence of streams and branches, the one crossing the other so many times, and all fair and large, and so like one to another as no man can tell which to

take ... we were also carried in a circle amongst multitudes of islands, and every island so bordered with high trees as no man could see any further than the breadth of the river. . . . It was as dark as pitch, and the river began to narrow itself and the trees to hang over from side to side." The explorers had to cut a passage with their swords through the tangle of branches that hung over the water.

The journey had its compensations: "On the banks of these rivers were divers sorts of fruits good to eat, flowers and trees of such variety. . . . We saw birds of all colours, some carnation, some crimson, orange-tawny, purple."

The captured Indians took Raleigh and his party to an Indian village on the banks of the river. Unlike the Spaniards, who tortured the Indian men and abused the women, the Englishmen treated the local inhabitants with great friendliness. Raleigh insisted on it. He was so successful in his dealings with the Indians that when he was ready to depart they begged him not to go. At the request of one of the chiefs, he later took the man's eldest son back to England with him.

The expedition made its way out of the swamplands near the coast. Then they passed through the beautiful savannas of Guiana. Raleigh

Left: the mouth of the Orinoco River which led, according to Juan Martinez, to the fabulous gold mine of El Dorado. It furnished riches so great that even the sidewalks were paved with gold. It was up this river that Raleigh was determined to go, to find the mine.
Below left: an early map of the Orinoco, with the islands and "broken ground."

Below: Raleigh's party with friendly Indians, from an early account of exploration in South America. His policy toward the Indians was to treat them with humanity and honesty. He was repaid with help, courtesy, and respect from the people he encountered. It was a great change from the typical Spanish methods.

Right: a German map of the 1600's of South America, which shows the Orinoco and mentions the expedition under Raleigh. It is decorated with some of the creatures reputed to live in the interior. The artist knew of the Orellana expedition down the Amazon, for a woman warrior stands on the banks of the wide river next to a headless man, another popular legend of the Spanish.

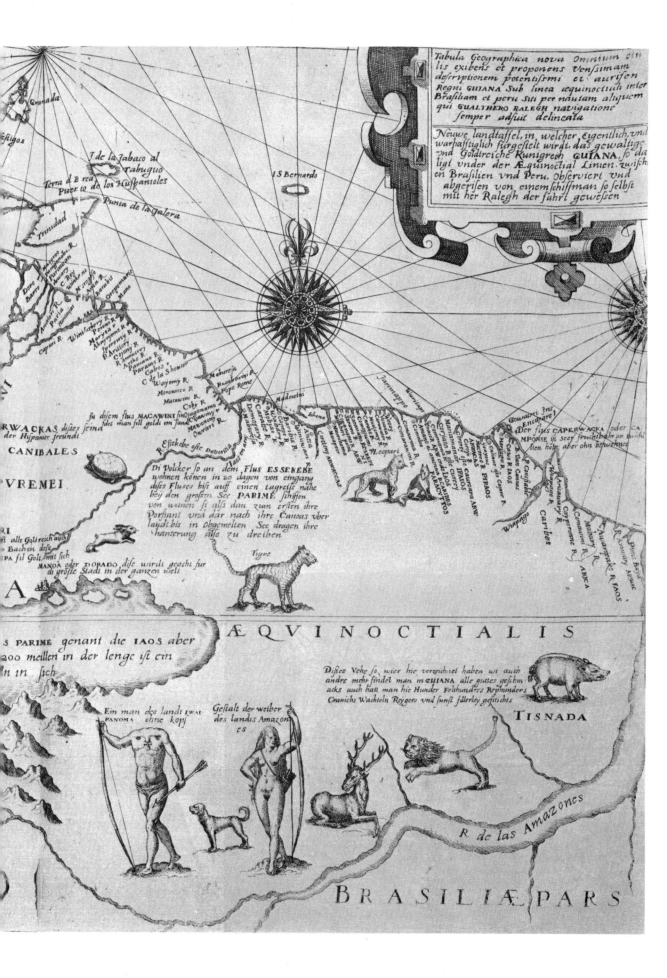

Above: an early picture of Indians melting down gold to make figurines in molds. After the fabulous wealth of the Inca Empire, Europeans could believe that even the most primitive American Indians might have enormous supplies of jewels and precious metals. But Raleigh was able to take only some gold-bearing ore back to England.

was impressed. "The most beautiful country that ever mine eyes beheld; and whereas all that we had seen before was nothing but woods, prickles, bushes, and thorns, here we beheld plains of 20 miles in length, the grass short and green, and in divers parts groves of trees by themselves, as if they had been by all the art and labour in the world so made of purpose. . . ."

Sailing up the broad mainstream of the river, which Raleigh estimated as nearly six miles wide, the crew dined on turtle eggs, wild game birds, and fish. At a small village by the riverside, Raleigh witnessed the suffering of a dying man who had been hit with a poisoned arrow. He observed that the Spaniards had never been able to get the Indians to tell them what the antidote to the deadly poison was ". . . although they have martyred and tortured I know not how many of them. But everyone of these Indians know it not . . . but their soothsayers and priests, who do conceal it, and only teach it but from the father to the son." The antidote was not to be discovered by Europeans for more than 100 years. Then it turned out to be very simple—common salt.

At the Caroni River, Raleigh took a detour. He had read of the cataracts that the first Spanish explorers had seen. From 20 miles away, he could see the frothing "breach of waters" that tumbled down from the highlands. "There appeared some ten or twelve overfalls in sight, every one as high over the other as a church tower, which fell with that fury, that the rebound of water made it seem as if it had been all covered over with a great shower of rain; and in some places we took it at the first for a smoke that had risen over some great town. . . ."

The crew returned to the main river. As they sailed, Raleigh's guides told him the same legends that had fascinated the first Spaniards. They talked of a strange race of men who had mouths in their chests and eyes on their shoulders. And they spoke of the Amazon women who in one month every year "cast lots for their valentines [husbands]."

But the fabled mine of El Dorado remained elusive. There was no sign of it at all. Then the rainy season on the Orinoco began to set in. "The fury of the Orenoque began daily to threaten us with dangers in our return. For no half day passed but the river began to rage and overflow very fearfully, and the rains came down in terrible showers and gusts in great abundance."

Reluctantly, Raleigh turned back toward the Atlantic Ocean. He had spent only a few months in the new land. He had got almost nothing out of it. His expedition had been outfitted at considerable expense, yet he was returning virtually empty handed. Leaving two men behind as English representatives in the territory, Raleigh gathered up as much gold-bearing ore as he could find to take back to England. He reasoned that, if tests on the amount of gold in the ore were favorable, he would be able to return to South America the following year to look for more. Raleigh did not suspect that it would be 20 years before he saw Guiana again.

In England, experts did indeed report favorably on the ore. But Raleigh's enemies at court would allow him no credit for the find. They claimed that he had never made the trip. They said he must have bought the ore from some other explorer. He pretended to have sailed abroad, they said, but in reality Raleigh had never left England.

In reply Raleigh wrote his book *The Discovery of Guiana*. It was an immediate and popular success and was translated into the principal European languages. But it failed in part of its purpose. Raleigh hoped that the queen would be sufficiently impressed by the book to outfit another expedition. She might even allow him to establish a colony in the new land.

But Raleigh had already established one ill-fated colony, the Virginia settlement of Roanoke. Now he was unable to convince the queen that greater wealth lay in extending the empire abroad than in war and piracy. He was too far ahead of his time. It is doubtful whether Elizabeth even bothered to read his book. Certainly she never commented on it. Those who did comment on the book accused Raleigh once again of lying. They would not believe that oysters grew on mangrove trees in Trinidad, that Amazon women lived in the South American interior, or that gold was to be found anywhere in Guiana. They said it was all an elaborate hoax.

So Raleigh tried another ploy to regain the queen's favor. In

Above: Robert Cecil, his signature and seals. Robert Cecil and his father, Lord Burghley, were powerful members of the courts of both Elizabeth I and James I, and enemies of Raleigh. Below: the frontispiece of Raleigh's *The Discovery of Guiana*, 1596, with which he hoped to impress the queen.

THE
DISCOVERIE
OF THE LARGE,
RICH, AND BEVVTIFVL
EMPYRE OF GVIANA, WITH
a relation of the great and Golden Citie
of Manoa (which the Spanyards call El
Dorado) And of the Prouinces of Emeria,
Arromaia, Amapaia, and other Countries, with their riuers, ad-
ioyning.

Performed in the yeare 1595. by Sir
W. Ralegh Knight, Captaine of her
Maiesties Guard, Lo. Warden
of the Stanneries, and her High-
nesse Lieutenant generall
of the Countie of
Cornewall.

Imprinted at London by Robert Robinson
1596.

league with the queen's favorite, Lord Essex, he led an attack on
the Spanish fort of Cádiz. But this expedition, too, was a failure,
and the invaders were routed. A year after their return, Essex led an
unsuccessful uprising against the aging queen. He was caught and
beheaded.

With Essex gone, Raleigh's most feared enemy at court was the
influential Sir Robert Cecil (later Earl of Salisbury). Cecil turned
several other powerful men against Raleigh. They set the stage for
the false accusation that eventually cost Raleigh his life.

Queen Elizabeth died in 1603, and on her death James I succeeded

Queen Elizabeth I of England had no children, and was succeeded to the throne by James VI of Scotland, son of Elizabeth's cousin, Mary Queen of Scots. James, who became James I of England, went constantly in fear of rival claims to the throne, and of plots to usurp his position as king, and he would act ruthlessly to put down intrigues against him. Here, Walter Raleigh is seen standing trial for an alleged conspiracy against James.

to the throne. Although the new king had never met Raleigh, his mind had been set against him by Raleigh's enemies.

Another English nobleman, Lord Cobham, was convicted of conspiring against the king. He claimed, falsely, that Raleigh was part of the plot. James, and almost everyone else, believed him. Cobham charged that Raleigh had taken money from the Spanish government to assist in deposing James. He said that Raleigh intended to influence a new monarch to relax the traditional English enmity toward Spain. The accusation roused public feeling against Raleigh.

Cobham later reversed his accusation of Raleigh. He went on to give so many versions of Raleigh's involvement that his word was obviously worthless. But it was enough for Raleigh's enemies. He was tried and duly convicted of treason.

The trial was a personal victory for Raleigh. When the court first convened, public opinion was totally against him. But Raleigh's brilliant defense in his own behalf convinced everyone of his innocence.

The public cried out for Raleigh's acquittal, but he was duly sentenced to death. Execution day was set for December 9, 1603. Then when the day dawned, King James made one of the dramatic gestures of which he was so fond. Just as the man named as Raleigh's co-conspirator was about to put his head on the block, word came that the king had stayed the order of execution for both men. Raleigh, then 51, was led away to the Tower of London, where he was to spend the next 13 years.

With no other distractions, Raleigh turned once again to writing. In prison he researched and wrote his six-volume *History of the World*.

In 1616, King James's avaricious nature won out over his vindictiveness. Several recent expeditions to Guiana, one of them partly financed by Raleigh, had revived the legend of El Dorado. Raleigh was set free by the king to find it. Although not immediately pardoned, Raleigh was told that he would be if he succeeded in finding the gold mine.

But Raleigh's second South American expedition was doomed from the start. For one thing, Raleigh was now an old man. He had suffered a stroke in prison, and now walked with a limp. He was further weakened by recurrent bouts of a liver ailment. Even more discouraging were the conditions that King James imposed on the voyage. During Raleigh's long imprisonment, a Spanish-English alliance had been made.

James was now actively wooing England's former enemies. He even wanted to marry his son to the Spanish princess. He was anxious, therefore, that Raleigh should not jeopardize the alliance by antagonizing Spain. Thus, the explorer departed with an impossible task. His mission was to search for gold in a territory that Spain claimed as its own. Yet he was not permitted to engage in anything that Spain might term a hostile act. Even if the Spanish

Above: in spite of the triumph of his trial, Raleigh was sentenced to death and only reprieved on the appointed day of execution. He was then locked up in the Tower of London, where he is shown here, with his family. He spent the next 13 years as a prisoner there studying and writing.

Left: the frontispiece of his six-volume *History of the World,* which he was permitted to publish in 1614.

provoked them and fired first, Raleigh was not to retaliate.

To assure the Spaniards of his good intentions, James made Raleigh draw up an itinerary of his South American journey. Without informing Raleigh, he gave an exact copy of the document to the Spanish ambassador in London. The Spanish knew in advance exactly where Raleigh would go, and they were able to lay a trap for him. The Spanish ambassador, Gondomar, remembered the Englishman's early exploits against Spain. He was opposed to Raleigh's South American venture and used every opportunity to poison King James's mind against him.

Only the chance discovery of great wealth could have saved Raleigh. The odds seemed to be against it. Nevertheless, he set out full of hope. With him on the journey were his son Walter, a man of 24, and his friend Keymis who had gone on the first expedition.

Above: the Tower of London, facing the Thames River, during the 1600's. The square building in the center, with the flag flying, is the original Tower, built by William the Conqueror.

Things went wrong from the start. Scheduled to sail in May, 1616, the ships were hemmed in by a succession of bad storms on the south coast of England until late August. On the voyage to South America, half the ships' crews were stricken with fever. As they left the Canary Islands, Raleigh himself contracted the fever and spent 28 days in delirium. Before they finally reached the delta of the Orinoco, 42 of the crew had died.

Too weak as a result of the illness to explore the river himself, Raleigh sent Keymis and Walter to do the job for him. He instructed them to go 400 miles up the Orinoco to where he thought the legendary mine of El Dorado might be.

Keymis ignored Raleigh's orders. He decided instead to attack the Spanish village of San Thomé, which was some distance upriver and which was rumored to have another gold mine nearby.

❧ By the King.

❧ A Proclamation declaring His Maiesties
pleaſure concerning Sir Walter Rawleigh, and
thoſe who aduentured with him.

Hereas We gaue Licence to Sir Walter Rawleigh, Knight, and others of Our Subiects with him, to vndertake a Voyage to the Countrey of Guyana, where they pretended great hopes and probabilities to make diſcouery of certaine Gold Mines, for the lawfull enriching of themſelues, and theſe Our Kingdoms: wherein We did by expreſſe limitation and Caution reſtraine, and forbid them and euery of them, from attempting any Acte of hoſtility, wrong, or violence whatſoeuer, vpon any of the Territories, States, or Subiects of any forraine Princes, with whom Wee are in amitie: And more peculiarly of thoſe of Our deare Brother the King of Spaine, in reſpect of his Dominions and Intereſts in that Continent.

All which notwithſtanding, we are ſince informed by a common fame, that they, or ſome of them haue, by an hoſtile inuaſion of the Towne of S. Thome (being vnder the obedience of Our ſaid deare Brother the King of Spaine) and by killing of diuers of the inhabitants therof, his Subiects, and after by ſacking and burning of the ſaid towne, (as much as in them for their owne parts lay) malitiouſly broken and infringed the Peace and Amitie, which hath beene ſo happily eſtabliſhed, and ſo long inuiolably continued betweene Us and the Subiects of both our Crownes.

Wee haue therefore heldit fit, as appertaining neerely to Our Royall Juſtice and Honor, eftſoones to make a publique declaration of Our owne vtter miſlike and deteſtation of the ſaid inſolences, and exceſſes, if any ſuch haue beene by any of Our Subiects committed: And for the better detection and clearing of the very trueth of the ſaid common fame; Wee doe hereby ſtraitly charge and require all Our Subiects whatſoeuer, that haue any particular vnderſtanding and notice therof, vpon their duety and alleagiance which they owe Us, immediately after publication of this Our pleaſure, to repaire vnto ſome of Our Priuy Counſell, and to diſcouer and make knowne vnto them their whole knowledge and vnderſtanding concerning the ſame, vnder paine of Our High diſpleaſure and indignation; that wee may thereupon proceede in Our Princely Juſtice to the exemplary puniſhment and coertion of all ſuch, as ſhal be conuicted and found guilty of ſo ſcandalous and enormous outrages.

Giuen at Our Mannor of Greenwich, the ninth day of Iune, in the ſixteenth yeere of Our Raigne of England, France and Ireland, and of Scotland the one and Fiftieth.

God ſaue the King.

¶ Imprinted at London by Bonham Norton, and
Iohn Bill, deputie Printers for the Kings moſt
Excellent Maieſtie.
Anno M.DC.XVIII.

Left: James I wanted the wealth of the New World, but wanted an alliance with the Spanish as well. Raleigh's commission was, therefore, to perform an impossible task—to search for gold in territory the Spanish claimed, but not to offend them while doing so. When Keymis was unwise enough to disregard the orders, James I issued this proclamation of his displeasure.

Right: the execution of Sir Walter Raleigh after his unsuccessful attempt to find the gold of El Dorado. James I used the earlier conviction of treason and had him beheaded in 1618.

Keymis' plan went wrong. The Spanish got wind of the impending attack and attacked the English first. Forced to retaliate, the invaders marched into the town. Walter recklessly led the English forces in fierce hand-to-hand fighting. Within minutes his lifeless body lay in the street. Keymis eventually succeeded in taking San Thomé. But no gold mine was found nearby. As far as Raleigh's agreement with the king was concerned, the damage had been done. The Spaniards wasted no time in sending back word of the fighting. Long before Raleigh turned back toward England, his fate was sealed.

Keymis returned to Raleigh's ship. Heartbroken over the death of his son, Raleigh, in despair, upbraided Keymis for his part in the battle that had killed young Walter. Keymis found Raleigh's

wrath unbearable. He left Raleigh's cabin saying "I know then, sir, what course to take." Minutes later a cabin boy found him lying across his bunk with a knife through his heart.

Filled with grief over the dual tragedy, the explorer turned his ship toward England. But even as he sailed for home, Ambassador Gondomar was urging James to turn Raleigh over to the Spanish to be hanged. In the end, James decided to reserve the honor for himself. Unable to make a convincing case against Raleigh for the failure of his South American journey, James's court once again invoked the 1603 treason conviction against him. It was the same false accusation for which he had served so many years in the Tower. Raleigh was sentenced to die in October, 1618. This time there was no reprieve.

Measuring the Globe
4

The Ecuadorian province of Pichincha is distinguished by its climate. Stretching across a number of the highest peaks in the Andes, it contains some of the coldest and some of the hottest regions in South America. At the crest of its 19,000-foot mountains the temperature plunges far below zero. In the sweltering jungle valleys it soars to over 100°F. The province of Pichincha is also notable as home of Quito, the historic capital of Ecuador. Its other claim to fame is the important line that bisects it—the equator (called in Spanish *equador,* from which the country gets its name).

Over the centuries, Pichincha has figured in some of South America's most memorable moments. During the 1400's, it was an important Inca stronghold. In the 1500's, it was the departure point for Orellana's expedition. In the 1600's, Pichincha was the site of the famous battle of the Ecuadorian wars of liberation.

In the year 1736, Pichincha was the site of an undertaking that had nothing to do with conquest and was only secondarily concerned with exploration. A group of Europeans gathered there at the start of an unusual mission. They had come to determine the exact shape of the earth.

Scientists had known for centuries that the world is round. The voyages of Columbus and Magellan had confirmed the fact beyond doubt. But there was still considerable disagreement about exactly how round.

In the early 1700's, the English philosopher and mathematician Isaac Newton had theorized that the earth was an *oblate spheroid.* In other words, he saw it as being near-spherical, but flattened at

Left: Charles Marie de la Condamine, the scientist chosen by the French Academy of Sciences to make a survey that would enable calculations to determine the exact length of a degree of longitude at the equator. He made his measurements in the Andes range.

Right: a meeting of scientists around a globe. The whole question of the exact shape of the earth became an issue bitterly disputed on both sides.

the poles and bulging in the center. Newton thought that the bulge was the result of the earth's being tugged outward by the combined forces of the sun and moon.

His theory was disputed by the French director of the Paris observatory, Jacques Cassini. Cassini argued that the earth was a *prolate spheroid*. He described it as elongated at the poles and nipped in at the equator, looking "much as a pot-bellied man might [look if he pulled] in his girth by taking a few notches in his belt."

Over the years, the differences in opinion about the shape of the earth had caused a serious rift in the scientific community. Tempers flared and friendships were severed as scientists took sides on the issue. The only way to decide the matter once and for all was to make on-the-spot surveys. As a result of such surveys, scientists would be able to determine the exact length of a degree of longitude. Then the circumference of the earth at its center and poles could be measured and the argument fairly and finally concluded.

Left: Isaac Newton. His theory was that the earth was nearly spherical, but flattened at the poles and bulging slightly at the equator. This was disputed by Jacques Cassini, who said that it was elongated at the poles and nipped in at the equator. The argument arising from the two rival theories could only be settled by actual measurements taken on the spot.

Above: Chilean street vendors. The French scientists were charmed with their first experiences in Cartagena, where the townspeople were welcoming and hospitable. They found the colorful streets particularly exotic.

In the 1730's, the prestigious French Academy of Sciences decided to finance two major expeditions whose purpose was to make the required measurements. One would go to Lapland to measure the circumference of the earth through the North Pole. The other would go to the equator. A French scientist named Charles Marie de la Condamine was chosen to lead the second group.

Superficially, La Condamine seemed an unlikely choice for the head of such an important expedition. The handsome, 34-year-old aristocrat was as versed in the language of the salon as in that of the laboratory. He was a favorite guest at the court of Louis XV and a close friend of the writer Voltaire. He was, too, a charming escort sought after by some of the most beautiful women in Europe.

But for all that, in the field of science La Condamine was no mere dilettante. He was an accomplished mathematician, and a talented astronomer and student of *geodesy,* the science of earth measurement. Moreover, he had an intense intellectual curiosity and a fervent enthusiasm for discovery. At 29, unusually young for the honor, he had been elected a member of the French Academy. In its service he had already been on an expedition to the north coast of Africa.

The 10-man geodesic expedition sailed from La Rochelle on the west coast of France on May 16, 1735. Their mission took almost a decade. They spent a full nine years surveying the 200-square-mile

section of the Andes that represents two degrees of latitude. Their work involved climbing from lush jungles to snow-swept plateaus. They spent days signaling to one another with mirrors, from mountain peaks dozens of miles apart, in order to get accurate measurements. At the end of their stay they had collated the thousands of calculations needed for the precise series of triangles that gave them the measurement they sought—the arc of the meridian. But the expedition took its toll in lives as well as time. Three of its members did not return.

Among them, the nine men who set out with La Condamine had a wealth of learning in different scientific spheres. The party included a mathematician, Louis Godin, and an astronomer named Bouguer.

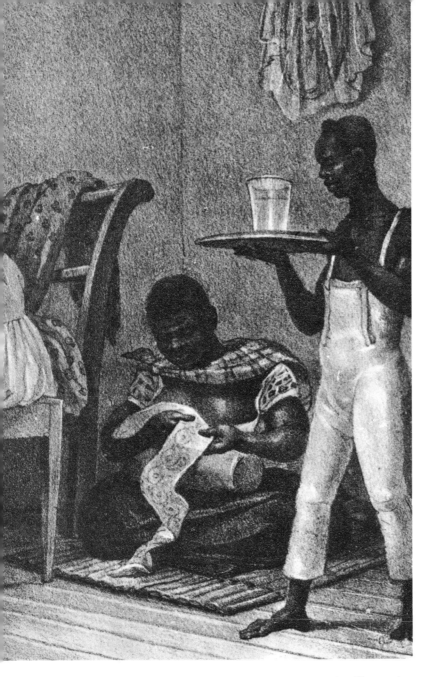

Above: one type of insect that would have pestered La Condamine and Bouguer along the coast.
Left: slaves—both local Indians and imported Negroes—made a languid and lazy life possible for the wives and daughters of colonial planters and businessmen. Lacking European cultural or educational opportunities, women—according to La Condamine —simply dawdled their time away.

There was a botanist, Jussieu, a draftsman, De Morainville, and a physician, Jean Seniergues. In addition, there were Godin's cousin, two technicians, and Monsieur Couplet, the nephew of the treasurer of the French Academy.

The voyage was uneventful, and the expedition sailed into Cartagena, Colombia, to an overwhelmingly enthusiastic reception. For weeks the group was wined and dined and feted by the aristocracy. Everyone they met was curious to hear more about the Frenchmen's intriguing mission.

The scientists spent happy days roaming the palm-shaded, perfumed streets of the port city, where the scent of vanilla mingled with the odor of sweet flowering shrubs. They saw street vendors wheeling wagons filled with native fruits they had never seen before—sapote, papaya, guayaba, and pineapples. They filled themselves with the delicious chocolates that were so expensive in Paris and so cheap in Chile.

La Condamine was fascinated by the relaxed way of life of the South American women, who led a life of almost total indolence. "In the house their whole exercise consists in sitting in their hammocks," he wrote in his journal. "In these they pass the greater part of the day." South American ladies also smoked cigarettes, a custom that had not yet caught on among Europeans. Many of the ladies even rolled their own.

La Condamine was anxious to get on to Pichincha. But he had not reckoned with the slow pace of life in the South American colonies. There were few timepieces, he observed, and his hosts seemed reluctant to commit themselves to planning for the future. "Soon" and "tomorrow" were the closest La Condamine could get to a specific commitment for departure. What had been planned as a brief visit extended to a lengthy stopover. It was February, 1736, before the expedition left Colombia to cross Panama and then sail along the foggy coast to Bahia de Manta, Ecuador.

Once there, the expedition split up temporarily. While the majority set off on the circuitous coastal route southward to Guayaquil, La Condamine chose to remain on the coast with Pierre Bouguer to study the area.

Theirs was an unhappy alliance. The astronomer was intensely jealous of La Condamine, although the count learned of this only later from a book Bouguer wrote about the trip. Their 170-mile trip up the coast to the equator was marked by constant arguments.

Insects swarmed about their heads as they trudged across the sand La Condamine described huge flying cockroaches the size of mice, hoards of mosquitos, and piume flies that sucked blood. Worst of all were the chiggers, burrowing insects that lay their eggs under the skin of human feet.

The main point of open contention between the two men was the route they were to follow to join their companions. La Condamine wanted to canoe up the Esmeraldas River to Quito. Bouguer wanted to take the already familiar, well-traveled, but roundabout route through Guayaquil.

The two men spent two months of suffering and bickering,

Right: a rubber plant, *Hevea brasiliensis Euphorbiaceae.* Before La Condamine's journey, rubber had never been seen in Europe, although Cortes and other Spaniards had remarked on this strange bouncing substance. La Condamine watched the Indians tapping the rubber trees for their sticky white sap, and learned how they made it into waterproof cloths. The Indian word for the tree was *cauchuc.* In French the word became *caoutchouc,* which now means rubber goods generally.

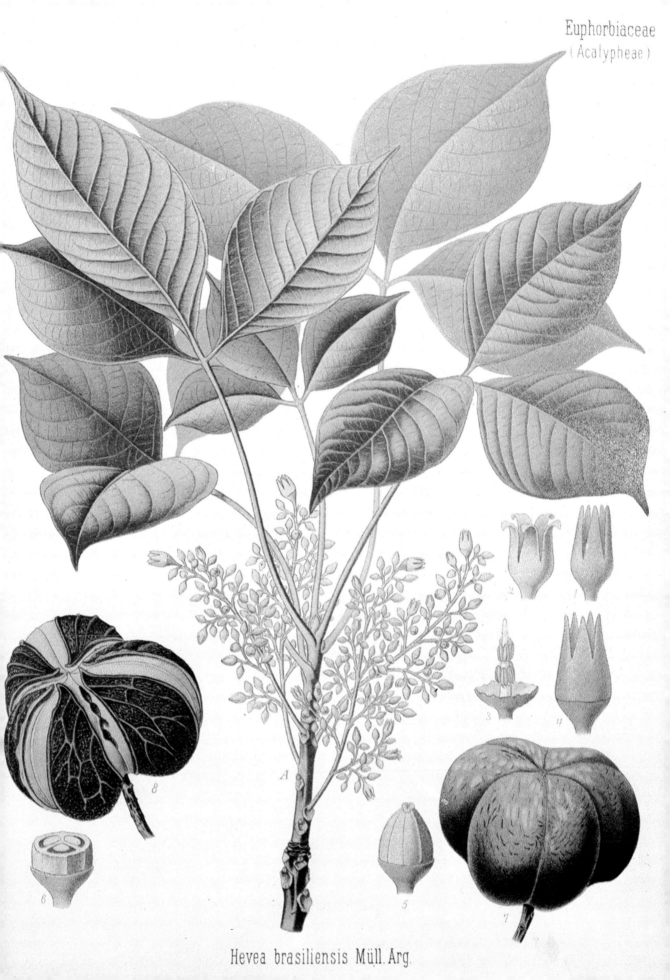

Euphorbiaceae
(Acalypheae)

Hevea brasiliensis Müll. Arg.

struggling all the while to make accurate measurements in spite of the thick fogs that blanketed the coast. Then chance stepped in to shape their future. One evening as La Condamine and Bouguer worked in their tent on the Cape Pasado Peninsula, three men rode into the camp. One of them was a South American named Pedro Vincente Maldonado.

Hearing about the French expedition from friends in Panama, Maldonado had determined to track down its leader. As well as being a keen mapmaker, Maldonado was a mathematician and, like La Condamine, had a keen curiosity about almost everything scientific. He was a native of Ecuador and spoke French, Spanish, and the local Indian tongue. He was just then engaged in opening up for general commerce the very route that La Condamine hoped to follow to Quito. He had already persuaded the Spanish authorities in Venezuela to build a road part of the way from the Esmeraldas through the Andean rain forest.

So Bouguer left to follow the others along the high road through Guayaquil. La Condamine and Maldonado, meanwhile, pushed north along the low Esmeraldas route, through the country that yielded the fabulous gems that the Spaniards had murdered for. It was now May, 1736, exactly a year after La Condamine's departure from France.

After following the coast north, the men entered the mouth of the Verde River and traveled inland in a 40-foot dugout canoe. When they were not busy correcting and enlarging their maps, the two men explored the teeming jungles around them, making the first accurate scientific observations on the tropical vegetation and wildlife.

They dined on beans, rice, and bananas, and drank a native alcoholic drink called Masato-sum, made from fermented plantains. Then, after journeying inland for a few weeks, La Condamine discovered the substance that was profoundly to influence the course of history in South America and in the world—rubber. Centuries before, Cortes had written about the strange bouncing balls with which the Aztec played. Other Spaniards had since described in their journals the substance of which these were made. But La Condamine was the first to experiment with rubber and to carry samples of it back to Europe.

In an Indian village in Esmeraldas province, the naturalist watched

Above: a drawing of Quito, much as it was when La Condamine and his group of scientists were there. Isolated from the world by ridges of the Andes, the people of Quito were completely provincial in their ideas and attitudes.

Below: a reception of the kind with which the nobility of Quito welcomed the French scientists. But suspicion followed sharply on the heels of hospitality when they observed the scientists' mysterious activities.

as Indians tapped hollow sticks into some of the trees and caught the sticky white sap in dried gourds. The Indians called it *jebe* and fashioned the rubber into waterproof cloths called *caoutchoucs*. Henceforth, La Condamine carried his instruments in a waterproof pouch made from two of the cloths.

Farther up the river he and Maldonado unknowingly discovered another important substance—a metal that looked like a cross between gold and silver, which the Spaniards called *platino*. Years later, European metallurgists analyzed the new metal and named it platinum.

The two men were now approaching the Puerto de Quito—so named by Maldonado, who established the village at the beginning of his new road over the mountains to the capital. During their first evening there, La Condamine met some colorful Colorado Indians who dyed themselves bright red from head to toe. The Indians, all friends of Maldonado, agreed to act as guides to the explorers through the vast rain forests that blanketed the lower slopes of the Andes.

As the men climbed higher, the misty warmth of the tropical rain forest gave way to the cloud forest and then to the dwarf forest. At 3,000 feet up, the Colorado Indians began to shiver with cold, so Maldonado sent them back to the village. Now La Condamine and Maldonado climbed up to the cold Puna region. Only coarse grass, cactus, and lichens could survive at such a height. La Condamine measured their altitude again. They were 12,000 feet above sea level.

The city of Quito nestles between mountain peaks in an *altiplano*, a natural area of fertile plains that lies between the eastern and western ridges of the Andes. The inhabitants of the city had heard word that the group of scientists was on its way. When the whole party had assembled, the scientists' lives became a round of receptions, balls, and fiestas. The members of the nobility of the city tried everything to outdo one another in generosity.

But the hospitality was short-lived. The upper class citizens of Quito were almost all uneducated, mercenary, and provincial in outlook. It was hard for them to believe that anyone would work as hard as the Frenchmen did for the sake of knowledge alone. Rumors began to circulate about what the men might really be doing.

Day after day, the townspeople watched as the scientists worked on the windswept plains above Quito, taking measurements for the baseline for their first triangle. At night the temperature dropped below freezing. During the day it soared to over 100°F. All the scientists became ill as a result of exposure to the harsh climate. Yet they still managed to drag their surveying chains across the inhospitable terrain. Then Couplet became so ill with fever that he could not leave his bed. The others watched helplessly as he grew weaker and weaker. A few weeks after their arrival, he died.

Couplet's death was a personal tragedy for the other members of the expedition. But for the people of Quito it was a choice morsel of gossip. The young man's death fed the rumors that were spreading through town. People were saying that the scientist's surveying instruments were really witching sticks—sticks believed to have magical powers—for ferreting out buried Inca treasure. The death of Couplet was rumored to be the outcome of bitter internal squabbles among the group.

The gossip became more and more vicious. Soon government officials began a daily harassment of the scientists at the site of the survey, exhausting them with constant questioning. Finally the situation grew unbearable. La Condamine was forced to travel to Lima, in Peru, to plead with the viceroy there for permission for the group to continue their work uninterrupted. The interlude cost the expedition eight months of valuable time.

Right: a Quito street scene. The city, surrounded by mountains, was quite beautiful, and the streets were busy and lively, but even the foremost citizens at the time of La Condamine's visit were uneducated and superstitious, ready to believe the most improbable rumors about the French scientists.

66

When La Condamine returned, he had permission and additional funds from the viceroy toward the continuation of the work. But official sanction did nothing to dispel the rumors. During two more years of surveying, the townspeople continued to gossip.

"Some consider us little better than lunatics," wrote a Spanish mathematician named De Ulloa who joined the group, "others impute our whole proceedings to the fact that we are endeavoring to discover some rich minerals or buried treasure."

Nearly four years after the group's arrival in the New World, the

. Loge où était Senergues avant le tumulte.
. l'Alcalde D. Sebastien Serrano } Chefs du tumulte.
. D. Nicolas de Neyra.
. D. Diego de Leon.
. D. Juan Ximenez Crespo G.ᵈ Vicaire de l'Evêque
. D. Mathias de la Calle Maj or de Cuenca, faisant ses efforts pour contenir la populace.
. D. Vincent de Luna y Victoria anc. Corregidor.
. D. George Juan Commandeur de S.ᵗ Jean de Jerusalem Lieutenant de Vaisseau de S. M. C.
. Le Curé de la G.ᵈᵉ Eglise de Cuenca, divers Ecclesiastiques et plusieurs de la Compagnie Fran

idle gossip led to tragedy. The expedition's physician, Seniergues, thinking he was doing a favor for a family friend, unwittingly became involved in a local scandal.

Weeks before, Seniergues had agreed to act as a go-between in a romantic affair involving the daughter of the prominent Quesada family—descendants of the conquistador. Their pretty daughter Manuela had been jilted by her fiancé, Diego de Leon. In the society of the time, his faithlessness doomed her to spinsterhood. As partial compensation, the Quesada family wanted De Leon to settle a sum

Above: a colonial girl with her head and face modestly covered by her mantilla. When Manuela, the daughter of the Quesada family, was rejected by her fiancé, she was considered doomed to lifelong spinsterhood.

Left: the death of Dr. Seniergues, when he was mobbed by a crowd at the local bullfight. In this illustration from La Condamine's book, *A* shows the doctor. *a* marks the box of the Quesada family where he had been watching the bullfight, *B* and *C* are the leaders of the mob, and *D* (on extreme left) indicates Diego de Leon, who, by his jilting of the Quesada girl, Manuela, had led to the whole situation.

1. L'Eglise de St Sebastien de Cuenca.
2. Cimetiere de l'Eglise et Parc des Taureaux destinés pour la fête.
3. Eglise principale sur la Gde place de Cuenca.
4. Eglise des Jesuites.
5. Eglise des Dominicains.
6. Eglise des Religses de la Conception.
7. Balcon d'une partie des Academiciens François, et de leur Compagnie.
8. Montagnes de Vavalchuma et autres qui bornent l'horizon de Cuenca.

69

LETTRE

A

MADAME ***

Sur l'Emeute populaire excitée à Cuen-
ça au Pérou, le 29 d'Août 1739,
dans laquelle fut assassiné le Sieur Se-
niergues, Chirurgien du Roi; nommé
pour accompagner MM. de l'Acadé-
mie des Sciences, envoyés par le Roi
en 1735, pour aller mesurer les de-
grés terrestres sous l'Equateur.

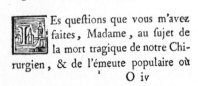 Es questions que vous m'avez
faites, Madame, au sujet de
la mort tragique de notre Chirurgien, & de l'émeute populaire où
O iv

Above: the title page of *Letter to
Madame ****, in which La Condamine
tried to explain to the shocked French
scientific world and the public how
the respected Jean Seniergues came
to be involved in such a tragedy.

of money on her at least to assure her financial security. They asked Seniergues to relay this wish to her former fiancé.

The doctor did so, only to learn later that De Leon had been extremely insulted by the request. Not only did he refuse to give Manuela any money, but he accused Seniergues of having an affair with her. The accusation enraged the doctor, who challenged De Leon to a duel. But when he arrived at the appointed hour, he was met by an angry crowd, who disarmed him. By now everyone had taken sides against the Frenchman—even the town priest, who read sermons denouncing the doctor and the expedition.

Courageously, Seniergues stuck by Manuela and her family. And a few weeks later, on August 29, 1739, he even dared to share their box at the city's bullfights. It was a fatal decision. The crowd around them was in an ugly mood, needing only a small spark to arouse their fury. Don Nyera, a friend of De Leon's, provided it. Approaching the Quesada box, the man shouted an insult at Seniergues. When the doctor rose to shout his reply, Nyera loudly accused him of threatening his life. The crowd exploded and surged on to the field.

The doctor stood facing them, alone, pistol and sword drawn. As his friends tried to go to his aid, they were held back by the mob. La Condamine and the others were forced to stand and watch while Seniergues was stoned and stabbed to death by the people who had entertained the whole group so graciously in the beginning.

La Condamine was horrified and heartbroken. He spent months in local courtrooms documenting a case against De Leon and Nyera. His efforts finally resulted in a verdict against them. But despite the conviction, the two men were not punished. The officers of the law were on the side of the murderers. And, in prosecuting them, La Condamine had brought the wrath of the town against himself.

The expedition worked on. There were now only seven functioning members of the original group. But the botanist Jussieu and one of the technicians had both become insane—Jussieu at the accidental loss of his entire plant collection, the technician as a result of severe illness.

By 1741, the greater part of the measuring work had been done. Then the group found itself embroiled in yet another local controversy. La Condamine called it "the war of the pyramids." The members of the expedition had decided to mark the baseline of their first triangle with two small pyramids. These were to be simple stone structures, bearing the French coat of arms and the names of La Condamine, Bouguer, and Godin. Nothing seemed more harmless to them. But the people of Quito saw the pyramids as an insult to their national pride. The French coat of arms was considered an insult to Spanish South America. Furthermore, there was no mention of the two Spanish scientists who had joined the expedition. The Frenchmen were ordered to tear the monuments down.

La Condamine went to court. After a year of legal battling he won the right to leave the pyramids standing. The only condition was that the Spanish names be inserted and the coat of arms removed.

The measurements had been completed, and the remaining members prepared to return to France. During the expedition's final weeks in the Andes there was another fatality. The draftsman, De Morainville, became the third to die. He was crushed under the crumbling walls of a church he was helping to build.

A few months afterward there was a happier incident. The mathematician Louis Godin announced that he was planning to marry a local girl, the daughter of a Venezuelan aristocrat. The scientists all attended the wedding. The occasion marked the end of their work in Pichincha.

A few weeks later, La Condamine set out with Maldonado on his voyage to the sea. Carrying the rough maps that the Spanish expedition under Orellana had made, the scientists left for Peru. They made their way down the Bracamoros River to the Marañón and from there on to the great Amazon itself. In the two-month journey to the Atlantic Ocean, they compiled a map so accurate that it remains largely unchanged today.

On the way downriver, La Condamine heard talk of a rumored link between the Amazon and the Orinoco via the Negro River. He wrote a detailed account of what he had heard. It raised questions that were not to be answered for a generation. The two naturalists were also the first to measure the depth, width, and speed of the river. They concluded that it was probably the largest in the world.

In the settlements they visited, La Condamine discovered the modern insecticide now called *rotenone,* an extract of the Barbasco plant. The local inhabitants threw it on the water to kill their fish so they could catch them easily. He studied the habits of sea cows, collected the seeds of the cinchona tree (from the bark of which quinine is obtained), and found a second antidote for the deadly poison curare. Sugar, he discovered, was just as effective as salt.

Early in the spring of 1745, La Condamine and Maldonado reached Paris. But the most amazing adventure of the La Condamine expedition was still to come. Louis Godin, the mathematician who married a Venezuelan girl, finally set out down the Amazon in 1749 to take ship to Europe. Wars and illness prevented him from going back to fetch his wife, and it was not until in 1769 that Madame Godin, with her two brothers, set out for the coast. Tragedy soon struck the party. Their native escort deserted, their canoe overturned, and all Madame Godin's companions died one by one in the pathless jungle. She alone staggered on until friendly Indians gave her food and assistance. Eventually this courageous woman joined her husband in Guiana after a 20-year separation. It was an astonishing achievement, and a fitting end to the adventures of the La Condamine expedition.

La Condamine died at the age of 73. The journals he left behind were filled with enough new surveys, experiments, and naturalistic lore to keep mapmakers and museums busy for another generation. And his diaries were spiced with enough romance, tragedy, and adventure to keep Europe reading and talking for another century.

Below: La Condamine's map showing the meridian at Quito. Although the group's aim was successfully achieved, the measurements they took are thought to be of less importance than the knowledge of the area gained. Plant and animal life were recorded, and discoveries of substances that have become part of everyday life were made. The charts made by La Condamine and Maldonado as they sailed down the Amazon were so accurately compiled that they can still be used today.

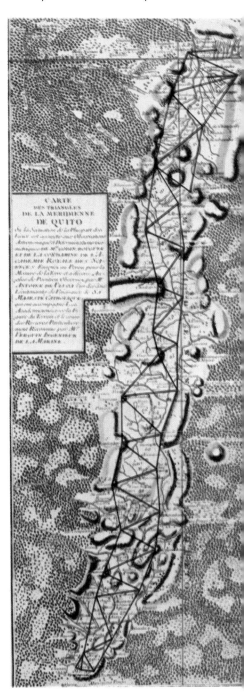

CARTE DES TRIANGLES DE LA MERIDIENNE DE QUITO

Above: Alexander von Humboldt in 1796, when he was 26 years old. Ambitious and intelligent, he decided to continue the work of La Condamine in South America, and set himself a program of studies in languages and the natural sciences in preparation.

A New World for Science
5

High above the valley of the frothing Chama River in western Venezuela two glacier-capped granite mountains reach toward the sun. These are the Humboldt Peak and the Bonpland Peak.

Few people today know the story of the men they are named for. But in the 1800's, their names were household words throughout the civilized world. Everyone had heard of the two naturalists Alexander von Humboldt and Aimé Bonpland. They were almost as famous a pair as Don Quixote and Sancho Panza or Tom Sawyer and Huckleberry Finn. Their adventures were certainly just as extraordinary. But they were fact, not fiction.

Von Humboldt was born into an aristocratic German family. As a schoolboy and student he acquired an encyclopedic knowledge of the natural sciences, and an unquenchable curiosity. Bonpland was born in France. He had trained as a physician, and was an expert and enthusiastic botanist. Between them the two men opened up a whole new world for science.

Their laboratory was the vast South American continent. In the interests of scientific discovery they trudged the dusty pampas, navigated treacherous rapids, hacked their way through the jungle, and groped along the icy ledges of some of the highest peaks in the

Above: a picture from Von Humboldt's own book showing himself and Bonpland in South America. The two men made an enormous contribution to knowledge of the continent, organizing their new discoveries in a coherent, scientific form that is still the foundation for current studies of the area.

73

Above left: Von Humboldt surrounded by botanical equipment. Although he had some knowledge of botany, he was no expert and needed a botanist to accompany him. Above right: Aimé Bonpland, physician and enthusiastic botanist. His accidental meeting with Von Humboldt led to a six-year expedition, and a lifelong friendship.

Andes. Von Humboldt's discoveries and observations fill more than 20 volumes. Bonpland cataloged 3,500 new species of plants—almost doubling the number previously known in the whole world. Dozens of plants bear Bonpland's name. Von Humboldt's has been given to a North American mountain chain, a Pacific Ocean current, three varieties of mineral, a California lily, and a national park.

Since childhood, both men had eagerly sought the opportunity to explore a new continent. An unlikely series of events brought them together and made their journey possible.

From the age of 10, Von Humboldt had cherished the dream of following La Condamine's footsteps across South America. In preparation, he had schooled himself in French, Spanish, and Latin and had read widely in all the sciences. As a young man, he had to bow to his mother's wishes and pursue the traditional family career in the civil service. He was employed as chief surveyor of one of Germany's mining districts. Von Humboldt was not excited by the work, but he learned a great deal from it, and became an expert geologist and topographer. Later, he trained himself to climb mountains in the Alps. He used his surveyor's instruments to calculate the heights of the peaks he had climbed. With his geologist's tools he analyzed the rock strata.

When his mother died, the baron, by now 25 years old, was free to pursue his dream. His mother left him a large inheritance, sufficient to equip an expedition to South America. But before he could set out, Von Humboldt had to find a botanist to go with him to share the work. Botany was one field in which he was not an expert.

For a time, it looked as if Von Humboldt had come up against an

Above: a view of a small volcanic eruption. It was in the Canary Islands, during a stopover on the trip to Cuba, that Von Humboldt and Bonpland climbed down into the crater of the volcano Pico de Teide and took readings of the temperature there.

insurmountable obstacle. In a year of traveling through Austria and Germany he did not meet any qualified scientists willing to undertake the journey with him. When he reached Paris in 1799, Von Humboldt gave up his search. Instead he accepted an invitation to travel to Egypt. To prepare himself, he planned to study archaeology in the libraries and museums of Paris.

Von Humboldt settled down in Paris. Then, as he was returning to his hotel one night, he encountered the man who changed his plans and his life. Von Humboldt bumped into Aimé Bonpland on the stairway of the hotel where he was staying. Had he not seen the case that the man carried over his arm, Von Humboldt would probably have brushed past with a brief apology. But Bonpland was carrying a botanist's specimen box. Immediately interested, Von Humboldt introduced himself. He learned that Bonpland was a doctor, a year out of medical school. He learned, too, that Bonpland cared far more about plants than about medicine.

Below: northwest South America, showing the routes of the members of the French expedition under Bouguer and La Condamine between 1735 and 1744. Particularly impressive is the amazing distance traveled, much of it alone, by Madame Godin, wife of the mathematician Louis Godin, on her way back to the Atlantic coast in 1769. Also shown are the routes followed by the German scientist and explorer Von Humboldt in the years 1799-1803.

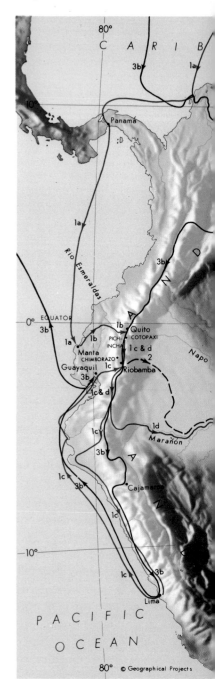

This chance meeting on the hotel stairs was the beginning of six years of adventure and a lifelong friendship. A few weeks later, the two men set off to Madrid. There the baron charmed his way past court intermediaries and gained an audience with the Spanish king. Delighted with Von Humboldt's knowledge of Spanish etiquette and impressed by his mining expertise, the monarch decided to offer the two scientists passage and protection to South America. In exchange for official permission to travel anywhere on the continent, the men promised to bring him back reports of mineral deposits and precious metals.

Von Humboldt and Bonpland set sail for Cuba, in the Caribbean, from the port of La Coruna, in northwest Spain, on the afternoon of June 5, 1799. Their first problem was getting out of harbor. Napoleon was preparing for war against England, and the ports of Europe were being attacked by the English fleet. In order to elude several English warships that were blockading the harbor, the ship's captain picked a time when no one would expect him to try to depart. They set sail in the midst of a howling gale. High winds had driven the English far off shore, and the captain seized the opportunity to head his ship, the *Pizzaro,* out of port. Rolling and pitching dangerously close to the rocks the ship made for the open sea.

During their 41-day voyage, Von Humboldt and Bonpland worked and studied from dawn till dusk. They searched for fish. They collected seaweed, dissected jellyfish, and managed to discover a new variety of alga (water plant). During a stopover in Santa Cruz, in the Canary Islands, the two scientists climbed the volcano Pico de Teide and descended its crater. Four thousand feet above sea level they were astonished to find that the temperature in the cracks of the volcano wall was 200°F. "The sulphur fumes burned holes in our clothes," wrote Von Humboldt, "while our fingers turned stiff with frost in a temperature of 12°F."

A week out from the Venezuelan coast, as passengers and crew sweltered in the fierce equatorial heat, they learned that a number of the steerage passengers on board had gone down with fever. Within a few days there was a raging epidemic on board. Bonpland, the ex-medical man, at once took over as ship's doctor. Finding that there was no supply of quinine with which to treat the patients, he advised the captain to change course and head for the nearest port.

70°   60°   50°

A N   S E A

A T L A N T I C

3a

3a

Caracas 3a Cumaná   1d   10°

3a

O C E A N

Apure San Fernando 3a
                              Orinoco

HUMBOLDT PK.
BONPLAND PK.

Atures Rapids 3a

Paramaribo

3a

1d

Atabapo
R.   Orinoco

3a   Canal
          Casiquiare

Mouths of the
Amazon   EQUATOR 0°

Negro

2   Pará
                              (Belem)

Negro

2
              Amazon   1d
1d   Amazon   1d

Manaus

10°

———— La Condamine (with Godin, Bouguer, & scientific party)	1a 1735–6
———— La Condamine (with Bouguer & Maldonado)	1b 1736
———— La Condamine	1c 1737
———— La Condamine (with Maldonado)	1d 1742–4
– – – – Madame Godin	2 1769–?
———— Humboldt (with Bonpland)	3a 1799–1800
———— Humboldt (with Bonpland)	3b 1801–3

70° 0   100   200   300   400   500   Miles 60°   50°

Left: one of the dry, dusty plains across which Von Humboldt and Bonpland trudged on their way from Venezuela to the Orinoco River. Typically, they made detailed observations of the plant and animal life found on the journey by pack train.

Right: a bat, *Stenoderma chilensis*. Von Humboldt's pet puppy was bitten by a vampire bat at one of the camps they had set up along the Apure River.

Below: the boat on the Guayaquil River, from Von Humboldt and Bonpland's book. In fact their boat was apparently much less protected than the craft shown here, since the men mention traveling in an open boat during the day, and having to stop to camp on shore at night. The river, appearing tranquil here, was actually a hazardous place, with enormous crocodiles lying along its banks as they passed.

They made for Cumana, in northeastern Venezuela. Months later, the naturalists learned that the shipboard epidemic had probably saved their lives. Cuba, their original destination, had been in the grip of a far more terrible scourge—bubonic plague (called the black death).

To amuse himself during the long voyage, Von Humboldt had been plotting the ship's course using charts of his own devising. He had discovered that the French, English, and Spanish navigational charts, all of which had been in use for the past 300 years, were wrong. Contradicting the captain's reckoning, the naturalist predicted that they would sight land on July 15. Von Humboldt was right. On July 16, the *Pizzaro* reached Cumana harbor, three days ahead of the captain's estimate. In the weeks after landing, the baron spent his spare time surveying the coastline. As a result of his labors on board and on shore he produced the first accurate maps ever made of the northeastern part of the South American coastline.

The activities of the voyage set the tone for the expedition ahead. Almost everything Bonpland and Von Humboldt did was to have major repercussions. Most of their observations either corrected old errors or led to important new discoveries.

After spending a few weeks in Cumana, the two men loaded their supplies aboard pack mules and headed for the mountains. Soon they were trudging west along the narrow trails on the high pass leading to the town of Caracas. From there they would go south across the grasslands to the village of San Fernando on the Apure River, a tributary of the Orinoco. After that they intended to take to the water. Their destination was the Orinoco River itself. Their purpose was to find the point where the Orinoco joins the Negro River and links up with the vast Amazon system.

On the way, Von Humboldt and Bonpland studied the grass and trees in the dry, dusty savanna near San Fernando. They learned that in the flood season the entire area becomes a great inland sea, studded with hummocks of dry ground. And they came across a tree of the mulberry family, called a "cow tree" and took samples of its milk-like juice, which both provides nourishment and quenches thirst during the long summer.

One day, Von Humboldt and Bonpland stopped to bathe in one of the mudholes that dot the plains during the dry season. Later they learned that they had been fortunate to escape injury. The ponds were full of electric eels, which the locals called *trembladores*. Curious to study these eels, Von Humboldt offered a reward to any Indian who could bring him a specimen.

Next day, they watched as the Indians drove a team of horses into a pool of eels to exhaust their electric force. The horses went mad with pain. They reared and plunged blindly through the muddy water. Some collapsed stunned, and drowned. When it appeared that the eels had been rendered harmless, the Indians speared them and pulled them out onto the bank.

Walking over to one of the writhing creatures, Von Humboldt

placed his foot on its tail. He was thrown backward by a shock that kept him in intense pain for hours afterward. Nothing daunted, he and Bonpland dissected one of the eels and discovered the fibers that give the animal its electric power.

The two naturalists began their journey down the Apure in a riverboat that had skins stretched across the stern for tables and seats. Traveling in an open boat by day, sleeping under the stars in a rope hammock at night, the two men were soon covered with painful insect bites. In the evening, jaguars growled ominously in the darkness beyond the campfire. At one camp, Von Humboldt was stalked by a jaguar and his puppy was bitten by a vampire bat. The pet was later killed by another pair of jaguars.

If their boat had ever overturned, the two explorers would have met certain death from the ugly giant crocodiles that lined the shore. Von Humboldt measured several of these that were more than 20 feet long. Naturalists have since ascertained that the Orinoco crocodile is the largest in the world.

In spite of the ever-present crocodiles, it was mainly pleasurable appreciation, not apprehension, that marked the river journey. Brilliant yellow-green and blue macaws added their staccato cries to the muted calls of bellbirds and doves. Wild hogs, sea cows, and tapirs swam in the muddy waters. Bush-dogs and maned wolves roamed the undergrowth. Sloths and opossums hung from the trees. Giant anacondas wrapped themselves almost invisibly around trunks and tree limbs. As the men drifted downriver, bright butterflies glided beside them. From time to time saki (cotton-top) monkeys would swing unexpectedly across the ship's bow on hanging vines. Both men made notes and sketches of all the animals and birds they caught sight of.

In March, 1800, eight months after their landing at Cumana, Von Humboldt and Bonpland reached the Orinoco. There, Von Humboldt began making the first accurate survey of the river's width. The reading was $2\frac{1}{2}$ miles. But the river's width changed with the seasons. During their three-month journey, spring came to the upper Amazon basin. Seasonal flooding then swelled the Orinoco to a width of seven miles. It was still no match for the Amazon, however, which widens to more than 50 miles during the rainy season.

The naturalists were astonished by the lushness of the rain forest that surrounded them. Comparing it to European forests, Von Humboldt wrote: "The earth, overloaded with plants, does not leave them room for growth. The trunks of the trees are everywhere covered with a thick carpet of verdure. . . . The same lianas, which creep along the ground, rise to the tops of trees and pass from one to the other at a height of more than 100 feet."

At a small island on the upper Orinoco, the explorers witnessed the annual turtle egg harvest. Each year, thousands of the lumbering, 150-pound reptiles gathered during the dry season to lay their eggs on the river sandbars.

The *turtle butter* (oil from the eggs), was a cooking staple among

Above: a drawing of a plant, *Rhexia sarmentosa,* by Aimé Bonpland. Using careful, scientific methods, Bonpland nearly doubled the number of plant species known in the world at that time by cataloging 3,500 new species.

Right: Von Humboldt and Bonpland at a camp in the Orinoco forest. They had reached the river in March, 1800, and both had immediately set to work. Von Humboldt made the first accurate survey of the river's width while Bonpland continued with his plant collecting.

the local inhabitants. Baby turtles were considered a great delicacy. Von Humboldt and Bonpland watched as the Indians dug the eggs out of the sand and piled them into empty canoes. Then they mashed them with sticks and poured water over them. The oil rose to the surface to be skimmed off and stored in large vats. Six thousand eggs were destroyed to make one gallon of oil. Von Humboldt estimated from the harvest he witnessed that more than a million turtles nested on the island, laying 100 eggs each.

A few days' journey above the waterfalls of the Orinoco, the two

Left: cooking in a riverside camp. The conditions along the Orinoco River made life thoroughly uncomfortable without the added difficulties of meticulous scientific research that both men resolutely continued. Their diminishing supplies meant a monotonous diet of rice mixed with large ants, with only bananas and manioc roots for change.

men paused to transfer their belongings to a dugout canoe. It was the only kind of boat that could navigate the Orinoco's treacherous rapids. From here to the Negro River the two would sit hunched inside a hollowed-out log 30 feet long but only 3 feet across. As well as the two naturalists, inside the frail craft were their Indian guides. and a large collection of rare animals.

The naturalists had been warned against going any farther on the treacherous river. Some 50 years before, a Spanish expedition of 325 men had lost their way searching for the spot where the Orinoco

joins the Negro. All but 13 of them had died. But Von Humboldt was confident of success. He knew that the Casiquiare, a stream that linked the two rivers, had been. successfully navigated 200 years earlier by the Spanish soldier Lope de Aguirre. The stream's existence had been confirmed by another traveler, Cristobal de Acuna, in 1639. Von Humboldt was convinced that the trip could be made quite safely.

The rapids were not their only obstacle. By now the insects had become almost unbearable. The men's feet were abscessed from chigger bites, and they had to sleep buried to the neck in sand to

Above: the Negro River in Brazil. The scientists had no difficulty in recognizing its inky waters, which were in marked contrast to the yellow, mud-colored waters of the Pimichin that flowed into it. During their journey on the Negro, the scientists watched Indians brewing the deadly curare poison and were allowed to take samples away with them—an acquisition that nearly cost Von Humboldt his life.

escape the bites of malaria-carrying mosquitos. Bonpland was fighting a losing battle to save his plant collection. Specimens not destroyed by mildew were chewed up by ants. The botanist was finally forced to heave dozens of cases of his carefully pressed plants into the river.

The food the explorers ate became less and less appetizing. Their normal menu was large ants mixed with rice, with only bananas and manioc roots to relieve the monotony.

On the way upriver at Atures, the Orinoco rises more than 50 feet in a 7-mile stretch of roaring rapids. The explorers had to carry their canoes across the mossy, foam-drenched cliffs. Beyond the rapids, the Orinoco veers eastward, and the naturalists turned off it on the small Atabapo River. From there, they proceeded to the Pimichin River, and, a few hours later, finally reached the Negro River. There was no mistaking the great river. Its dark waters contrasted sharply with the mud-yellow Pimichin. Farther downstream, where the Negro River joins the Amazon at Manaus, the difference is even more pronounced. At their junction, it looks as if a line has been drawn across the river mouth. The waters of the two rivers finally mix miles downstream.

Once on the Negro River, Von Humboldt and Bonpland journeyed on to the Casiquiare. Father Acuna had said that it circled back to the Orinoco. At its headwaters, the baron stopped to plot their position 2°0'4" above the equator. The legendary river link had been conclusively established and charted.

Warned against venturing into hostile Portuguese territory to the south, the two men decided against following the Negro to the Amazon. Instead, they retraced Acuna's route and headed back toward Cumana.

Their outward journey had been filled with adventure. They had stayed at a remote Indian village with a Spanish priest who had not seen a white man for 10 years. They had encountered a Spanish-speaking white man living in a grass hut in the middle of the jungle—the man's father had been a Spaniard and he considered himself superior to the natives. "In that vast solitude," Von Humboldt wrote, "[there was] a man believing himself to be of European race and knowing no other shelter than the shade of a tree, yet having all the vain pretentions, hereditary prejudices, and errors of long-standing civilization."

Above: an Indian of the Mato Grosso, the great forest lands of western Brazil. Even today the interior is not completely mapped, and Indian tribes live as their ancestors have lived for generations, completely untouched by, and unaware of, the modern world.

Left: Amazonian Indians killing a
tapir. For the two naturalists, a
meeting with friendly Indians offered
more than a chance to expand
their ethnographical material. The
Indians would generously share the
results of their hunting expeditions,
making great feasts with the meat.

Left: a sketch of one of the thousands
of plants that Bonpland identified
for the first time. This one was given the
scientific name *Melastoma coccinea.*

At one Indian village they had been invited to a banquet where the *pièce de résistance* was large apes, grilled whole on a turning spit.

Earlier, the scientists had been invited by villagers to watch the secret process of curare brewing and were allowed to take a few test-tubes of the poison with them. Their curiosity almost proved to be Von Humboldt's undoing. On the return trip to Cumana, a demented Indian guide tried to kill him. The Indian knew that the baron suffered from open sores on his toes and feet, and smeared the contents of a test tube of curare inside his shoes, hoping to poison him. Fortunately Von Humboldt noticed the sticky substance.

On the Orinoco once again, the naturalists visited the caves of the dead at Atoribe, collecting several skeletons as specimens. The Indians were horrified by their action. They believed that anyone who disturbed the skeletons faced certain death. The Indians' fears were almost justified. Before they reached Cumana, Bonpland nearly died from an attack of malaria and Von Humboldt became severely ill with typhoid.

Above: Mount Chimborazo from the Plain of Tapia. Von Humboldt and Bonpland climbed to within 1,500 feet of the summit, but were turned back by a chasm that they were unable to cross. But their 19,000-foot climb was the highest point reached by any men at that time.

Right: a botanical chart of Mount Chimborazo—a drawing from one of Von Humboldt's own books, showing the variety of plant life that he observed at different levels while on the climb. The cleft that prevented them from reaching the top is indicated at top right.

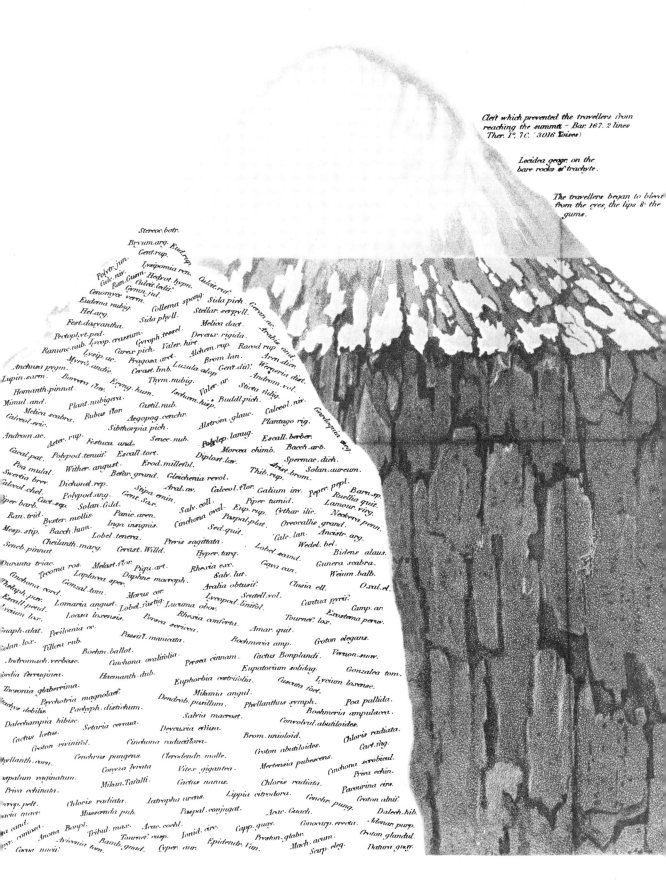

Cleft which prevented the travellers from
reaching the summit – Bar. 167. 2 lines
Ther. 1°. 7C. (3016 Toises)

Lecidea geogr. on the
bare rocks of trachyte.

The travellers began to bleed
from the eyes, the lips & the
gums.

Stereoc. botr.
Bryum.arg. Eudr.ap.
Gent.rup.
Polytr.jun. Lysipomia ren. Calcie.ria.
Calc.niv.
Ran.Gusm. Hedwot.hypn.
Gymn.jul. Calcie.ledif.
Cenomyce vern.
Eudema rubig. Collema spong. Sida pich. Geran.ac.
Hel.arg. Sida phyll. Stellar. serpyll. Arabis and.
Fest.dasyantha. Melica dact.
Pectophyt.ped. Deverx. rigida.
Ranunc.nub. Lycop.crassum. Gyroph.tessel. Valer. hirt. Alchem.rup. Racod.rup.aud.
Lysip. ac. Carex.pich. Fragosa arct. Brom.lan. Aren.dier.
Anchusa pygm. Myrti.andic. Cerast.Imb. Luzula alop. Gent.dif. Weigeria dist.
Lupin.sarm. Borrera flav. Eryng. hum. Thym. nubig. Androm.vol.
Homanth.pinnat. Plant.nubigera. Lochern.hisp. Valer. ar. Sticta ridig.
Mimul.and. Castil.nub. Buddl.pich.
Metica scabra. Rubus flor. Aegopog.cenchr. Calceol.niv.
Calceol.eric. Sibthorpia pich. Alstrom.glauc. Plantago rig. Gardoquia gry.
Androm.ac. Aster. rup. Festuca and. Senec.nub. Polylep.lanug. Escall.berber.
Cacal.pat. Polypod.tenuif. Escall.tort. Morea chimb. Bacch.arb.
Poa mulal. Wither. angust. Erod.millefol. Diplost.lav. Arist.brom. Spermac.dich.
Swertia brev. Dichond.rep. Befar.grand. Gleichenia revol. Thib.rup. Solan.aureum.
Calceol.chel. Cact.sep. Polypod.ang. Stipa enin. Aral. av. Calceol.flor. Galium inv. Peper. pepl.
Piper barb. Gent.star. Salv.coll. Piper tumid. Barn.sp.
Ran.trid. Byster. mollis. Panic.aren. Cinchona oval. Eup.rup. Cythar ilic. Ruellia quit.
Mesp.stip. Bacch.hum. Inga insignis. Paspal.plut. Oreocallis grand. Lamour.virg.
Seneb.pinnat. Lobel. tenera. Sed.quit. Calc.lan. Neckera penn.
Cheilanth.marg. Cerast.Willd. Pteris sagittata. Lobel.saind. Wedel. bel. Ancistr. arg.
Durانta triac. Tecoma ros. Melast.flor. Piqu.art. Hyper.tarq. Gava can. Bidens alaus.
Cinchona cord. Gonzal.tom. Laplacea sper. Daphne macroph. Rhexia ex. Salv. lut. Gunera scabra.
Thelyph.per. Lomaria angust. Morus cor. Aralia obtusif. Clusia ell. Weinm.balb.
Escall.pend. Loasa loxensis. Lobel.rustig. Lucuma obor. Lycopod.linifol. Scutell.vol. Oxal.el.
Lycium lox. Rhexia confertu. Cortua pyrif. Camp. ar.
Gnaph.alat. Perilomia oc. Persea sericea. Amar. quit. Exostema peruv.
Solan. lox. Tillan rub. Passifl. maniata. Boehmeria amp. Tournef. lox.
Andromach.verbasc. Boehm.ballot. Goton elegans.
Cordia ferruginea. Cinchona ovalifolia. Persea cinnam. Cactus Bonplandi. Vernon.suav.
Tacsonia glaberrima. Haemanth.dub. Eupatorium soliday. Gonzalea tom.
Radvs debilis. Psychotria magnolaef. Euphorbia cestrifolia. Cuscuta foet. Lycium loxense.
Dalechampia hibisc. Pachyph. distichum. Mikania angul.
Cactus loetus. Setaria cernua. Dendrob. pusillum. Phyllanthus symph. Poa pallida.
Goton rivinifol. Salvia macrost. Boehmeria ampulacea.
Phyllanth.corn. Cenchrus pungens. Deveuxia eilisa. Convolvul.abutiloides.
Sepalum vaginatum. Conyza lyrata. Clerodendr. molle. Brom. unioloid. Chloris radiata.
Priva echinata. Milium.Taralli. Vitex gigantea. Goton abutiloides. Cact.rig.
Corryp.pelt. Chloris radiata. Cactus nanus. Mertensia pubescens. Cinchona scrobicul.
Mussenda pub. Iatropha urens. Chloris radiata. Priva echin.
cand. Anona Bonpl. Paspal.conjugat. Lippia citrodora. Pavourina cirs.
comosa. Tribul.max. Arac.cochl. Acac.Guach. Cenchr. pung. Croton alnif.
Cocos nucif. Avicennia tom. Bamb.guad. Tournef. cusp. Ionid.circ. Capp.guay. Cinocrup.erecta. Dalech.hib.
Cyper.aun. Epidendr.Van. Preston.glabr. Adenar.purp.
Scurp. eleg. Mach. acum. Croton glandul.
Datura gray.

87

In Cumana, still weak from their bouts of fever, the naturalists packed up their specimens. They planned to send them back to Europe aboard four different ships. At Von Humboldt's insistence, Bonpland made a copy of his plant catalog to keep with him in case the original was lost at sea. The job took weeks, but was worth the trouble. The Spanish ship carrying the original plant portfolio and all the botanist's specimen cases did not reach Europe. Another ship carrying the birds, monkeys, and reptiles reached port, but the animals were all dead by the time they arrived in Paris.

With the Orinoco expedition behind them, Von Humboldt and Bonpland turned to mountain climbing. In 1802, his feet still raw from the abscesses he had acquired in the jungle, Von Humboldt led

the way across mist-shrouded Andean ridges. The trek took them from northern Colombia to Lima in Peru. In Ecuador, the two men climbed the towering Mount Chimborazo, the highest point in the Cordillera Occidental of the Andes Mountains. They came within 1,500 feet of the summit before a 60-foot chasm forced them to turn back. The 19,000-foot climb they achieved was still the highest undertaken by anyone up to that date. And they had done it without the aid of modern mountain-climbing equipment. Although many attempts were made, Mount Chimborazo was not scaled for another 72 years.

In Peru, the two men visited the ancient Inca city of Cajamarca. There they paid a call on the last descendant of the Inca emperor

Above: hot springs, one of the wonders of South America that the two men reported to the outside world. They found themselves famous—appreciated by the public for their spectacular discoveries, and by the scientific world for the deliberate accuracy with which the discoveries had been recorded.

Below: Alexander von Humboldt, as an old man, in his study in Germany. After his return to Europe in 1805, he spent much of his time compiling books from his huge collection of notes—his reports finally ran to over 20 volumes.

Atahualpa. Traveling to the coast, they climbed the white chalk cliffs and took samples of the guano that the peasants used to fertilize their fields. Von Humboldt also investigated the cold-water current that now bears his name. He concluded that the current was responsible for the damp, misty climate of the Peruvian coastal lowlands. Before leaving Lima, the Peruvian capital, he made the first exact geographical survey of the city's location.

In Guayaquil in southwest Ecuador, the naturalists witnessed an eruption of the volcano Cotopaxi. Then they sailed up to Mexico. The hospitality of the Mexican viceroy so impressed Von Humboldt that he spent a year writing a history of the country as a gift for him. His four-volume *Political Essay on the Kingdom of New Spain* is still a standard reference work.

Traveling on to North America, Von Humboldt spent three weeks as the guest of President Thomas Jefferson. By this time news of the naturalists' discoveries had reached North America and Europe. Von Humboldt and Bonpland were famous.

In 1805, the two friends sailed for home. In the ensuing years, Von Humboldt became a sought-after lecturer and best-selling author. Bonpland was given a pension from the French government and for some time worked as an overseer in the garden of the Empress Josephine.

Later, Bonpland traveled to Argentina to set up a plantation. One of the crops he grew competed with a commercial crop grown by the mad dictator of Paraguay, Rodriguez Francia. Enraged, the dictator had Bonpland taken prisoner. He spent 10 dreary years confined to the small Indian village of Santa Maria. The Frenchman filled his time by caring for the sick and supervising the work of the palace gardeners.

It was 1829 before Bonpland was finally freed and allowed to go home. Von Humboldt, then 60 years old, returned from a tour of Russia for a final reunion with his friend in Europe. Then Bonpland went back to South America. Just before his 70th birthday he married an Indian woman.

Bonpland died in 1858. A year later, Von Humboldt died. At the time of his death he was immersed in writing the fifth volume of a book called *Cosmos* that would "put the whole material world, everything we know today of the firmament and of life on earth, from the tiniest moss on a rock, into a single work."

Darwin in South America
6

In 1859, Charles Darwin, an English naturalist, published a book called *On the Origin of Species by Means of Natural Selection, or the Preservation of Favoured Races in the Struggle for Life.* The whole of the first printing of 1,250 copies sold out on publication day, and the book gave rise to a storm of debate.

In *The Origin of Species,* Darwin gave the facts on which he based his concept of natural selection—the sequence of gradual changes in plants and animals that enabled them to adapt and survive through countless generations. The book caused a revolution in biological science. With some modifications its principles and statements have since been accepted by many groups.

The portrait that survives of Charles Darwin is of a frail, introspective man. He is remembered as a sickly recluse who shrank from publicity and endured physical hardship only because of his devotion to science. During the last quarter of his life, Charles Darwin fitted this description. But as a young man, he was quite different.

The youthful Darwin was as much an explorer as a scientist. The observations he made on the Pacific Galápagos Islands later had immense scientific repercussions as the first links in a chain of thought that led him to his revolutionary theory. At the time, they were just another interlude in an exciting voyage of exploration. The voyage began on the coast of Brazil in 1832. And for the next two years the naturalist spent more time on land than at sea, roaming through the southern half of the South American continent.

Darwin traveled from the Brazilian highlands to the Argentine pampas, up the spiny Chilean Andes and down to the bleak, stormy shores of Tierra del Fuego. He rode with *gauchos,* the South American cowboys, chatted with Indians and *banditos*—half-breed outlaws armed with razor-sharp knives. He also wrote a journal about his adventures that is probably the most detailed chronicle ever published on the land and life of the period in that part of the world.

Darwin was just 23 years old when the ship he traveled in, the *Beagle,* anchored in the harbor of Rio de Janeiro, Brazil, toward the end of February, 1832. Darwin had left his home in England with his father's grudging permission. His father gave consent to the voyage only after Charles had managed to find a "man of common sense" who would approve the journey. To everyone's surprise Darwin's uncle, Josiah Wedgwood, the prosperous porcelain manufacturer, urged his nephew to go. He argued that the ex-

Above: a cartoon of 1882, showing Darwin as an old man, the final product in the evolution of the species, having progressed from the worm at the bottom. By this time Charles Darwin was famous around the world, his theories being hotly disputed and equally heatedly defended.

Right: Darwin in 1840, just after his voyage of exploration, in a watercolor painted by George Richmond.

perience would be educational for the young naturalist. Until then Charles Darwin had not distinguished himself at anything except hunting and riding.

Like Von Humboldt, Darwin had spent his youth collecting "all sorts of things, shells, seals, franks, coins, and minerals." But he had never excelled as a scholar. And just as Von Humboldt had been pushed into the traditional family occupation of the civil service, Darwin had been encouraged to do something "useful." Until he left England, the naturalist had been halfheartedly pursuing a career in the ministry of the Church of England.

H.M.S. *Beagle,* which was under the command of a Captain Fitzroy, had been commissioned by the British government to survey the southern coasts of the Americas, southern islands, and Australasia. The youthful Darwin had joined the ship's staff as honorary naturalist. The *Beagle* had left Devonport harbor in December, 1831. Darwin's initial elation was quickly transformed into an attitude of stoic endurance as he learned that his stomach refused to adapt to the sea. The first two-month leg of the voyage set the tone for the entire five-year expedition. Darwin's life aboard ship was to be marked by constant bouts of seasickness. The infrequent moments when he was well were spent in arguments about the morality of slavery with the ship's captain, who thought it an admirable institution.

It was a relief to Darwin when the *Beagle* finally sighted the coast of Brazil and headed for the port of Rio de Janeiro. Today, Rio is a bustling metropolis, with skyscrapers, a modern airport, and a burgeoning population of more than $4\frac{1}{2}$ million. When Darwin landed there in the 1830's, the seaport was a sedate, scenic gateway to a wide-open frontier. The city had been settled by Spanish grandees three centuries before. Its weathered limestone buildings and fragrant vine-wrapped *haciendas* (ranch houses) offered few clues to the untamed country beyond.

Left: H.M.S. *Beagle* lying at anchor in Sydney Harbour, Australia. The *Beagle* was a very small brig, only 90 feet long, but, at the time of Darwin's voyage, it carried over 70 people.

The interior of South America in the early 1800's was far wilder than the American West. The South American general, Simón Bolívar, had led the series of revolts that finally ended Spanish power in South America in 1824. Since then, the country had been in a state of perpetual revolution and was drifting toward the military dictatorships that have gripped it ever since.

Brutality was a way of life. Ranchers had to guard their vast *estancias* (cattle ranches) from constant attacks by savage Indians. The Indians burned the ranchers' houses, murdered their families, and drove off their cattle. In return, the landowners raided Indian villages and slaughtered every inhabitant. There was safety only in numbers. Ranchers traveled in groups to fend off the Indians and the banditos. On every road the banditos might be hiding.

There was no police force or justice to speak of. Rich and poor followed an unwritten, and to an outsider, unfathomable, code of conduct. "It is curious that the most respectable inhabitants of the

Above: Bible reading on the *Beagle*. Captain Fitzroy was a devout Christian who believed confidently that the voyage would substantiate the story of creation as told in the book of Genesis. He trusted that young Darwin, as a naturalist, would inevitably discover many traces of the Flood.

Right: General Rosas, the commander of the army of Argentina. He had gained his position by virtue of his flawless horsemanship. His army was the only effective power in the land, and it was often brutal and ruthless.

country will invariably assist a murderer to escape," observed Darwin, "they seem to think that the individual sins against the government and not against the people."

The army was the only real law anywhere. Soldiers constantly roamed the prairies and highlands. They hunted down Indians and outlaws and stamped their own brand of brutality on an already cruel country. Treachery and bribery of government officials were commonplace. Survival depended on courage, cunning, and physical skill. In Argentina, General Rosas, the man who commanded the army, ran his camp like a king's court. He had been elected general not because of his intelligence or tactical skill, but because of his perfect horsemanship.

"An assembled army elected its general by the following trial," Darwin wrote, "a group of unbroken horses being driven into a corral, were let out through a gateway, above which was a cross-bar; it was agreed whoever should drop from the bar on one of these wild animals as it rushed out and should be able, without saddle or bridle, not only to ride it, but also to bring it back to their corral, should be their general. . . . This . . . feat has . . . been performed by Rosas."

Few South Americans of the period worked regularly. When Darwin asked some peasants why, "one gravely said the days were too long; the other that he was too poor. . . . The number of horses and the profusion of food," he concluded, "are the destruction of all industry."

Education was virtually unknown, even to the upper classes. Most military officers were only just able to write their own names. The ignorance of the ruling gentry was virtually total. Darwin was astonished at the unsophisticated conversational level of his fellow guests at dinner parties he attended.

"I was asked whether the sun or earth moved, whether it was hotter or colder to the north; where Spain was and many other such questions," he relates. "The better informed well knew that London and North America were separate countries close together and that England was a large town in London. . . . They expressed, as was usual, unbounded astonishment at the globe being round and could scarcely credit that a hole would, if deep enough, come out on the other side."

During his first months in South America, Darwin explored the highlands around Rio de Janeiro. He traveled through the "intricate

Left: an Argentinian officer and a soldier. Skill with horses was their most valued attribute, and their code of conduct was little different from that of the outlaws they hunted.

Below: a ball at one of the government houses in Chile. In spite of the great elegance of social functions, even the upper classes were virtually illiterate, and they seemed completely unaware of the most basic scientific facts that any European would know.

wilderness" of lakes outside Mandetiba. He rode through great open pastures in the valleys, all of them studded with cone-shaped ants' nests 12 feet high. Often the road was "so shut up that it was necessary that a man should go ahead with a sword to cut away the creepers." Camping in the tropical rain forest of the Parana River Valley, Darwin observed: "In the evening it rained very heavily. As soon as the rain ceased, it was curious to observe the extraordinary evaporation which commenced over the whole extent of the forest. At the height of 100 feet, the hills were buried in a dense white vapour which rose like columns of smoke."

During the long evenings, Darwin dissected glowworms to isolate their phosphorescent fluid. He made detailed notes on the habits of spiders, beetles, and other insects: "A person, on first entering a tropical forest, is astonished at the labours of the ants; well-beaten paths branch off in every direction, on which an army of never-failing foragers may be seen, some going . . . others returning, burdened with pieces of green leaf, often larger than their own bodies."

The hazards of traveling in South America were nearly matched by the discomforts. When there were no friendly estancias to stop at,

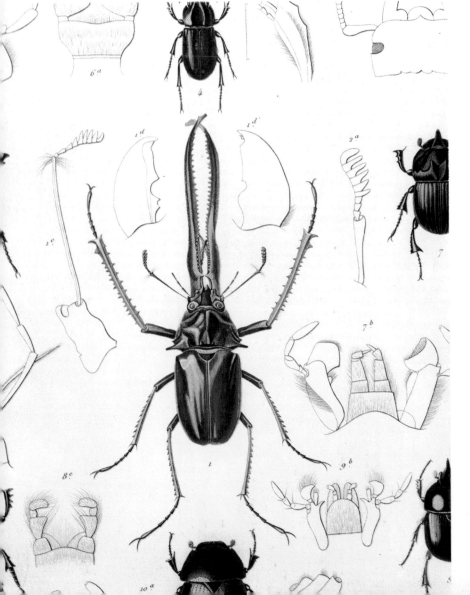

Left: Darwin used part of the time he spent in Argentina to make extensive notes on the insect life, observing and recording their habits with great care. This is a drawing of one of the beetles he saw, *Chiasognathus Granti.*

travelers had to take their chances at the local *vendas* (inns). The accommodation was a far cry from what a town-dwelling Englishman was accustomed to. The service was almost non-existent. "It not infrequently happened," said Darwin, "that we were obliged to kill, with stones, the poultry for our own supper."

From Rio, the *Beagle* headed south for the Rio de la Plata, the great bay formed by the Parana and Uruguay rivers. Ten miles off shore, the ship sailed into a cloud of butterflies. "Vast numbers . . .

Above: gauchos (horsemen) of the pampa, the wide prairie of the Argentine. It was men like these who accompanied Darwin on his overland journey from the Negro River. As a fine horseman himself, he was able to enter into their flamboyant, but harsh, life.

Left: the method of using the *bolas*, three leather-covered balls attached to a rope. It was thrown around an animal's legs to bring it down.

99

Darwin's voyage on the 'Beagle':

1a	27 December 1831 – 26 July 1832
1b	19 August – 2 November 1832
1c	26 November 1832 – 28 April 1833
1d	23 July – 3 August 1833
1e	6 December 1833 – 13 April 1834
1f	12 May – 23 July 1834
1g	10 November 1834 – 11 March 1835
1h	27 June 1835 ('Beagle' picks up Darwin on 5 July 1

Darwin's expeditions:

2a	19 January – 7 February 1833 (with small boats)
2b	mid 1833
2c	11–17 August 1833 (on horseback)
2d	8 – 20 September 1833 (on horseback)
2e	27 September – 7(?) November 1833 (on horseback and in small boat)
2f	14 – 28 November 1833 (on horseback)
2g	16–19 March 1834
2h	18 April – 8 May 1834 (with small boats)
2j	14 August – 27 September 1834
2k	22–28 January 1835
2m	13 March – 10 April 1835
2n	27 April – 4 July 1835

© Geographical

Above: Patagonian Indians, participants in some of the bloodiest encounters between colonists and Indians on the continent. Ranging across the pampas, each side ruthlessly murdered the other.

Left: southern South America, showing the journeys undertaken by the British naturalist Charles Darwin in the years 1831-1835. Darwin's observations on this voyage in H.M.S. *Beagle* provided him with the evidence upon which he based his famous work, *Origin of Species,* which he eventually published in 1859.

in bands or flocks of countless myriads extended as far as the eye could range. Even by the aid of a telescope it was not possible to see a space free . . . the seamen cried out 'it was snowing butterflies.' "

After making a speedy journey south from Montevideo, Uruguay, to Bahía Blanca, Darwin returned to Montevideo and set sail again almost immediately for the south. On this expedition he sailed all the way down the Patagonian coast to Tierra del Fuego and the Falkland Islands. Returning to Montevideo yet again, Darwin then journeyed east to Maldonado and made an exploratory trip into the inland region around about it. Later, he rejoined his ship and sailed south, passing Bahía Blanca to anchor in the mouth of the Negro River.

There are several Negro rivers in South America. The largest is the huge Amazonian tributary in northern Brazil. A second branches off the Rio de la Plata in Uruguay. And a third cuts across northern Patagonia about 300 miles south of Montevideo. The *Beagle* entered the mouth of the southernmost Negro River on July 24, 1833.

At this point Darwin decided to journey inland on horseback and rejoin the *Beagle* at Bahía Blanca. At first he had difficulty in getting any gauchos to go with him, but he was eventually able to persuade a small number to make the journey.

As they were approaching the coastal town of Bahía Blanca, Darwin and his party received word that soldiers manning a *posta* (small, manned fort) nearby had been murdered by Indians. A 300-man posse of soldiers was organized to pursue the attackers. Darwin describes the soldiers as more savage than the Indians.

Once hunted down, the Indians were to be massacred unmercifully, even the women and children. The thought of such bloodshed depressed and horrified Darwin. He predicted that the Indians would soon be exterminated. "The warfare is too bloody to last; the Christians killing every Indian and the Indians doing the same by the

Christians. It is melancholy to trace how the Indians have given way before the Spanish invaders."

On arriving at Bahía Blanca, Darwin decided, despite the danger of the area, not to rejoin the *Beagle* there and then. Instead he set out to cross the pampa and meet the ship at Buenos Aires, 500 miles away.

The pampa was bandito country, not a place for timid tourists. To venture out on the prairie, a man needed to be a crack rider with a lot of courage. Fortunately Darwin met the requirements. What he lacked as a sailor he made up for as a horseman.

Darwin greatly enjoyed the company of the gauchos he rode with.

He wrote about them with admiration: "Their appearance is very striking. They are generally tall and handsome, but with a proud and dissolute expression of countenance. They frequently wear... mustaches and long black hair curling down their back.... Their politeness is excessive... but whilst making their exceedingly graceful bow, they seem quite as ready, if occasion offered, to cut your throat."

The gauchos were all excellent horsemen and always gave the appearance of controlling their mounts effortlessly. "I have seen an animal bounding with spirit, yet merely reined by a forefinger and thumb, taken at full gallop across a courtyard, and then made to wheel round the post of a verandah with great speed, but at so equal a distance that the rider, with outstretched arm, all the while kept one finger rubbing the post," wrote Darwin.

Soon the gauchos taught Darwin how to rope an animal with a lasso and how to throw the *bolas*—leather-capped balls attached to a rawhide rope that entwined an animal's legs and brought it down. A really skilful rider could topple a rhea or a steer at 100 yards.

Darwin was already beginning to ask some of the questions that led his logical mind to conclusions that later rocked the religious world. Before leaving England, he had read a controversial book called *Principles of Geology* by Sir Charles Lyell. The author was one of the first scientists to make public his doubts of Biblical claim that the earth had been created in seven days. Lyell said that geological changes must have occurred over much longer periods of time—probably many millions of years.

Everything Darwin saw on the various stages of his South American journey convinced him that Lyell was right. The flat, desolate Patagonian countryside reminded the naturalist of what he had read about the Siberian flatlands of Russia. "In both countries, the salt lakes occupy shallow depressions in the plains. In both, the mud on the borders is black and fetid ... and the lakes are inhabited by small crustaceous animals and flamingoes.... As these circumstances, apparently so trifling, occur in two distant [places] we may feel sure that they are the necessary results of common causes...." Like Siberia, he concluded, "Patagonia appears to have been recently elevated above the waters of the sea."

Building on the idea of geological evolution, Darwin began to

Above: some of the animals of South America, from a French atlas. The curious ability of animal life to adapt to the conditions in which it lives—even to such hostile surroundings as the near-polar land of Tierra del Fuego—made Darwin ask himself some of the questions that led to his conclusions about evolution.

Right: the yagouarourdi, one of the strange creatures that Darwin found on the desolate plains of the pampas.

Above: three species of palm trees found in Argentina. During the long ride along the coast to Bahía Blanca, Darwin observed numerous palms.

apply its principles to biology. The ability of animal life to adapt to the harsh environment of Patagonia intrigued him. "Well we may affirm," he wrote, "that every part of the world is habitable, whether lakes of brine, or . . . the upper regions of the atmosphere and even the surface of perpetual snow . . . all support organic beings."

Patagonia and the pampa to the north of it had been the scene of the bloodiest Indian wars on the continent. The army, under Rosas' command, had made a great sweep through the countryside, slaughtering entire tribes. In an attempt to secure the area permanently, the soldiers had set up a series of postas on the plain. As fast as an outpost was established, the Indians wiped it out.

The naturalist was amazed and amused by the animals he encountered on the desolate plain. There were foul-smelling skunks, larger than polecats, who feared "neither man nor beast." There was an acquisitive rodent called a *bizcacha* with a habit of "dragging every hard object to the mouth of its burrow. Around each group of holes, many bones of cattle, dry dung, etc. are collected into an irregular heap . . . for what purpose . . . I am quite unable to form even the most remote conjecture."

At night, pumas and foxes prowled the pampa, frightening away herd animals being driven to market. "It is very difficult to drive

animals across the plains, for if in the night a puma . . . approaches, nothing can prevent the horses dispersing in every direction," he wrote, "an officer left Buenos Aires with 500 horses, and when he arrived at the army, he had under 20."

One evening the party ate a dinner of puma and rhea meat. The animals were killed in a violent storm that rained hailstones as large as small apples. Thirteen deer and dozens of small birds were also killed by the hail.

A few days out from Bahía Blanca, Darwin climbed the 3,500-foot Sierra de la Ventana, in east Argentina, a strange, solitary mountain of white quartz that looms above the flat plains. "The mountain is steep, extremely rugged . . . and so entirely destitute of trees, and even bushes, that we could not make a skewer to stretch out our meat over the fire of thistle stalks."

Darwin was always on the lookout for evidence to support Lyell's geological theories. Patiently he scoured the plain and river banks for hours on end, looking for fossils. On the shores of the Salado River, he found two near-perfect skeletons of the prehistoric rhinoceros and the remains of a mastodon, an extinct mammal.

When Darwin finally reached the outskirts of Buenos Aires, the capital city of Argentina, he found the city blockaded. A revolution

Above: the main plaza of Buenos Aires in the early 1800's. Darwin's arrival there coincided with a revolution and he had great problems in reaching the harbor where the *Beagle* was waiting.

had broken out. It was only with great difficulty that Darwin was able to get fresh horses to take him to the head of the Rio de la Plata. There he boarded a small boat to take him to Montevideo where the *Beagle* was now waiting. "This revolution [is] supported by scarcely any pretext of grievances," he wrote sarcastically, "but in a state which, in the course of nine months . . . underwent 15 changes in its government . . . it would be very unreasonable to ask for pretexts."

On another visit to Tierra del Fuego, the *Beagle* sailed south through the Strait of Magellan at the tip of the South American continent. There Darwin explored the dense, chill forests. "So gloomy, cold, and wet was every part that not even the fungi, mosses, or ferns could flourish."

In July, 1834, the *Beagle* headed up the western coast of South America to Valparaíso, in Chile. For several months Darwin explored the foothills of the Andes Mountains and hiked through the central highlands, returning to Valparaíso from time to time.

In February, 1835, going south toward the Chilean town of

Below: the remains of the cathedral in the ruins of Concepción, Chile. Descriptions of the quake, followed by a tidal wave, finally settled the case for geological evolution for Darwin.

Right: the town of Talcahuano and the port of Concepción, Chile, before the fatal earthquake on February 20, 1835. Darwin was at the time many miles to the south, at Valdivia.

Left: Darwin's tanager (a bird related to the Finch family) taken from a drawing in his book, *The Voyage of H.M.S. Beagle.* It was one of many birds first observed by Darwin and subsequently named for him.

Below: a caricature of Darwin in old age. His book was published 24 years after the journey that led to his theory on the origin of species

Concepción, Darwin had probably the most dramatic experience of his entire voyage. The day was February 20. Darwin had recently landed at the Chilean port of Valdivia. He was resting in the woods there, when the ground began to rock beneath him. "It was something like the movement of a vessel in a little cross-ripple," he wrote, "or still more like that felt by a person skating over thin ice, which bends under the weight of his body." The tremor lasted only a few minutes. A few days later the naturalist learned that the "tremor" was the most devastating earthquake to strike Chile in a century.

Two weeks later, the *Beagle* reached Concepción. Those on board were greeted by a scene of total devastation. "The ruins were so mingled together, and the whole scene possessed so little the air of a habitable place, that it was scarcely possible to imagine its former condition."

A mammoth tidal wave, a *tsunami* (the Japanese word for such waves), had followed the earthquake. It had completely wiped out the ruins of the neighboring village of Talcahuano. Survivors described it to Darwin. "A great wave was seen from a distance of three or four miles, approaching in the middle of the bay with a smooth outline; but along the shore it tore up cottages and trees as it swept onwards with irresistible force. At the head of the bay it broke in a fearful line of white breakers . . . two large vessels anchored near together were whirled about and their cables were thrice wound round each other; though anchored at a depth of 36 feet, they were for some minutes aground. . . ."

The earthquake tied the fragments of Darwin's previous observations together. He was convinced that his theory of geological evolution was correct. "We may confidently come to the conclusion," he wrote, "that the forces which slowly and by little starts uplift continents and those at which successive periods pour forth volcanic matter, are identical. . . . This rending and injection would, if repeated often enough, form a chain of hills. . . ."

In September, 1835, Darwin finally reached the Galápagos Islands. There, his observations of the Galápagos finches and other fauna led him to the theory of natural selection—the concept that in the struggle for existence some living things are better suited to live and have young, and that these survive where weaker things die or fail to reproduce. The phrase "survival of the fittest" is applied to this process of change by natural selection. This theory set the logical stage for the later theory of biological evolution. But it was not until 1854 that Darwin finally began to put the pieces of the puzzle together in his *Origin of Species.* It was published five years later. Darwin was then only 49. He was, however, already physically an old man. He was a semi-invalid as a result of a parasitical disease.

The naturalist continued to live and work until 1882, when he died at the age of 73. By then he had achieved worldwide renown, and his great theory assured that he would win immortality. But as the world mourned his passing, few remembered that the frail old genius had once had an equal talent for adventure.

LE BOTANISTE

Three Naturalists
7

Until the mid-1800's, the naturalists who explored South America had one important thing in common—a great deal of money. Von Humboldt and La Condamine had inherited wealth. And Darwin, while not rich, was comfortably off. But the next three naturalists to win fame on the continent were poor men. Two of them, Henry Walter Bates and Alfred Wallace, were both primarily concerned with entomology—the study of insects. The third, Richard Spruce, was a botanist. They began their exploration of the Amazon River Basin on a shoestring. All three were largely self-educated, and all three came from the British working class.

When Bates and Wallace met, they were both holding down what the average man in England of the time would have considered good positions. Bates was an apprentice to a hosiery manufacturer in Leicester, in the Midlands. Wallace, who had formerly worked as an apprentice land surveyor, was teaching mapmaking, geometry, and English at Leicester's Collegiate School. Spruce, meanwhile, was a mathematics instructor at another collegiate school, less than 100 miles north in York. Bates and Wallace did not meet Spruce in England. They met him by chance thousands of miles away in a small village in Brazil.

It was Bates's extensive collection of butterflies and beetles that first turned Wallace's interest toward natural history. Wallace was amazed, he later wrote in his book *Life,* at how many different kinds of insects were pinned beneath the glass of his friend's display cases. "If I had been asked before how many different kinds of beetles were to be found in any small district . . . I should probably have guessed fifty. . . . Now I learnt that there were probably a thousand. . . within ten miles."

Darwin had been influenced by the writings of Lyell. Bates and Wallace were tremendously impressed by a controversial book called *Vestiges of the Natural History of Creation.* Its author, Robert Chambers, had published it anonymously because of its controversial premise—that species could change and usually did.

Wallace, like many others, was disgusted with the inequality and general hypocrisy of English society. Specifically, he felt society had

Far left: a naturalist of the early 1800's. The fascination of a systematic study of nature—at first the prerogative of the rich—led Bates, Wallace, and Spruce all to hazard their slender means to travel to South America in search of new species.
Left: a page from Bates's notebook, with his sketches of butterflies from the jungle.

Right: Henry Walter Bates. When he met Wallace he was working for a hosiery manufacturer. He had always been very interested in natural history, and already had an extensive collection.

Far right: Alfred Wallace. He had been an apprentice land surveyor, and it was the money earned surveying for the railroads that financed the collecting trip to the jungles of South America.

caused the death of his older brother, who had died of pneumonia. For several years, Wallace had been longing to get away from England. Ironically, a symbol of the times, the English railroad boom of 1845, unexpectedly provided him with an opportunity to do so.

Railroad barons were encouraging speculators by mapping every likely spot on the English countryside that might support a railroad track. Experienced surveyors were much in demand, and their wages were high. In two years of surveying, Wallace was able to save a small sum of money. He wrote to his friend Bates in Leicester, to propose a collecting trip to South America.

It was a wild idea for two young men of such modest means to have. Bates's recollection of the incident, however, gives no hint of the excitement both must have felt: "In the autumn of 1847, Mr. A. R. Wallace, who has since acquired wide fame in connection with the Darwinian theory of natural selection, proposed to me a joint expedition to the River Amazons' (Bates always referred to it in the plural.)

The two naturalists sailed from Liverpool. They were the only passengers aboard the 192-ton barque *Mischief*. It arrived at the town of Pará (now Belém) at the mouth of the Amazon on May 28, 1848. "The appearance of the City at sunrise was pleasing in the highest degree," Bates wrote enthusiastically of Pará. "The white buildings roofed with red tiles, the numerous towers and cupolas of churches and convents, the crown of palm trees reared above the buildings, all sharply defined against the clear blue sky give an appearance of lightness and cheerfulness which is most exhilarating. The perpetual forest hems the city in on all sides landward; and toward the suburbs, picturesque country houses are seen . . . half buried in luxuriant foliage."

Bates was delighted with these first days in the port city. He wrote

Above: the coast of Brazil in the 1820's. Bates found his first sight of Brazil fascinating, and greatly enjoyed the port-city of Pará, where he and Wallace disembarked. They remained in and around Pará for a year before they were joined by Herbert Wallace and a botanist, Richard Spruce.

eloquently about the sounds, scents, and sights of the jungle. But Wallace, who had read a number of descriptions of South America and had expected something much more exotic, was disappointed.

During their first year in South America, Bates and Wallace explored the rivers and countryside around Pará. The following July, Wallace was joined by his younger brother Herbert. Herbert had sailed to Pará on the same ship as a botanist named Richard Spruce. Spruce, Wallace, and Bates decided to join forces.

Spruce, at 32, was the oldest and best educated of the naturalist trio. He was a student of Greek and Latin. On a collecting trip to the Pyrenees he had learned Spanish and French. He had also published several papers on botany. At home in England, Spruce had avidly followed Charles Darwin's adventures. For 10 years, a dull decade spent as a school teacher, he had been dreaming of an ex-

Above: Richard Spruce. He was 32 at the start of the expedition, and had long been planning a collecting trip to South America. It was made possible when the Royal Botanical Gardens in England agreed to help finance his journey.

pedition to South America. His passage to that country was being partly financed by the curator of Kew Gardens, the Royal Botanic Gardens in London, which contain the largest collection of living and preserved plants in the world. Bates and Wallace were also doing some collecting for the curator.

Leaving Bates at Pará to continue his collecting, Alfred Wallace, his brother Herbert, Spruce, and a shipboard acquaintance, Robert King, set out up the Amazon River for the city of Santarém, some 200 miles up the river from Pará.

After three months of collecting together in Santarém, the group broke up. Spruce settled down to spend a year collecting around Santarém. The Wallaces headed farther up river to what is now Manaus. On arrival at Manaus the Wallaces split up, Herbert returning to Pará, while Alfred caught a boat that was going up the Negro.

The Amazon basin was still virgin territory for collectors. Von Humboldt and Bonpland had collected some specimens, but had confined themselves to the Orinoco basin and the Negro, stopping short of the Amazon itself. La Condamine had taken specimens, including cinchona bark, back to Paris from the Amazon basin. Since then, few botanists had been there. Hundreds of plants were still unknown to science. And except for the larger species, the insects and wildlife were virtually unknown.

Bates left Pará and traveled to Manaus, where he met the Wallace brothers, before continuing up the Amazon to Ega. During his trip up the Amazon, Bates discovered hundreds of new insects and dozens of birds. He wrote of shooting three species of hawk, a Magoary stork, and two gilded-green Jacamars. He lived on a river boat, slept in a hammock on the foredeck, and ate by a campfire.

Spruce was astounded at the wealth of vegetation surrounding the city in which he was living. "There were enormous trees . . . decked with fantastic parasites, hung over with lianas which varied in thickness from slender threads to huge pythonlike masses. . . . Here our grasses are bamboos 60 or more feet high . . . . Violets are the size of apple trees."

During his stay at Santarém, Spruce inadvertently became part of a chain of events that was later to rob Brazil of her greatest asset—rubber. The curator at Kew Gardens had asked him to make a careful survey of all rubber-bearing trees so that experts could decide how best to transport them. Twenty years later, using the reports

Above: Bates being attacked by a flock of curl-crested toucans when he tried to capture one of them for his collection. He used this picture for the frontispiece of his book about his adventures in the Amazon region. Above right: a curl-crested toucan. When the group of four naturalists split up, Bates went up the Negro River where he sighted dozens of birds, which he recorded for the first time.

Spruce had written, a botanist named Henry Wickham took about 70,000 rubber-tree seeds back to Kew. With these seeds were founded the vast rubber plantations of Ceylon and Malaya.

But when Spruce laid the groundwork, rubber was little more than a curiosity. It was to be a decade before its uses in industry became fully realized. Then the rubber boom transformed South America.

Early in 1850, while Wallace was 1,000 miles up the Negro, Spruce received word of disaster in Pará. Epidemics of yellow fever and smallpox had struck the port-city. All river traffic between there and Santarém had been stopped. Thousands of townspeople were ill. Five hundred had already died. Spruce's concern was magnified by the fact that both Bates and young Herbert Wallace were in Pará. Bates had been forced to return there after a servant had robbed him of all his money. Herbert Wallace, finding his temperament unsuited

Above: a picture from Bates's book of one of his adventures—a midnight visitation from an alligator. He had to return from his river expedition when all his money was stolen by one of his servants.

to the slow, painstaking business of collecting, was awaiting passage back to England.

Spruce may have recalled one of the poems Herbert, who was an enthusiastic writer of light verse, had written about the constant, annoying swarms of mosquitoes on the river. "They murder gentle sleep, till . . . we've half a mind to weep." Herbert had added: "But still, although they torture, we know they cannot kill." In the mid-1800's, scientists were still unaware that mosquitoes carried disease. Herbert went down with yellow fever. Five days later he died. Bates, just recovered from an attack of the fever, took care of the boy during his illness. He slept by his side until Herbert died of the "black vomit." "At the time I fell ill," Bates wrote later, "every medical man in the place was working to the utmost in attending the victims of the other epidemic (smallpox); it was quite useless to think of obtaining their aid. . . ."

Alfred Wallace spent a year traveling up the Negro and Orinoco

Left: a drawing of two butterflies from the notebook in which Henry Walter Bates kept his field notes. After he was forced to return to Pará, Bates fell ill and was unable to continue his work. But he did gather strength enough to nurse the dying Herbert Wallace.

and back down the Negro River to Manaus. On the way, he had become so discouraged by persistent bouts of fever that he decided to return to England. News of his brother's death, which reached him at Manaus, confirmed his decision.

The fever, which may have been malaria, left Wallace fit for work only half of each month. "Every alternate day I experienced a great depression," he wrote, "this always followed a feverish night in which I could not sleep." Spruce, who was more than 100 miles upstream from Manaus on the Negro River, heard of Wallace's illness and went to his aid. Arranging for his friend's safe passage downstream to the coast, Spruce left Wallace. He promised to continue Wallace's interrupted studies on the Uaupés River, a tributary to the north and west of the Negro River.

On July 12, 1852, Wallace was finally helped aboard the small brig *Helen*. Below decks were cases of live animals he had collected. They included parrots, monkeys, and a forest wild dog. There was also his

Right: a giant buttressed tree of the sort that flourished around Santarém. As well as being impressed with the great variety of plants that had never been described before, the naturalists were astonished at the size to which familiar plants grew in South America.

entire collection of South American species of insects and birds—hundreds of them new to scientists at home. The cargo was worth enough to Wallace to support him for three or four years of collecting. But the ship did not reach London. Three weeks out, the *Helen* caught fire as a result of the careless packing of its flammable cargo. Instead of caulking up the hatches to smother the fire, the captain thoughtlessly opened them. The sea breeze fanned the flames.

After futile attempts to save his animals, Wallace climbed into the rescue dinghy and watched helplessly as the ship burned. "The flames very soon caught the shrouds and sails, making a most

magnificent conflagration. . . . Soon after, the fore rigging and sails also burnt. . . . If for an instant we dozed off . . . we soon woke up again . . . to see the red glare which our burning vessel cast over us. It was now a magnificent spectacle, for the decks had completely burnt away, and as it heaved and rolled with the swell of the sea, presented its interior toward us, filled with liquid flame—a fiery furnace tossing restlessly upon the ocean."

Wallace seemed more dispirited about the fate of his animals than about his own suffering. He wrote to Spruce about his feelings. "Several of the birds and monkeys, in trying to get away from the heat, retreated to the bowsprit, but the flames got them at last. Only one parrot was saved. He happened to have perched on a rope which swung down below the bowsprit, and when this burned, he fell into the water and was picked up. . . . Almost all the reward of my four years of privation and danger was lost."

The *Helen*'s survivors were picked up by a rotting, leaking vessel bound for England via Cuba. On October 1, 1853, the ship finally creaked into harbor at Deal, England.

Wallace's experience on the *Helen* was the prelude to a life that was filled with adventure, danger, and disappointment. Shortly after his return from South America, he sailed for the Malay Archipelago.

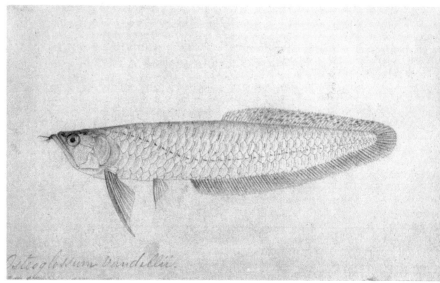

Right: drawings by Alfred Wallace of two of the fish that he discovered during his trip on the Negro River.
Above right: *Osteoglossium bicirrhasirm.*
Below right: *Acara viltata Hick.*

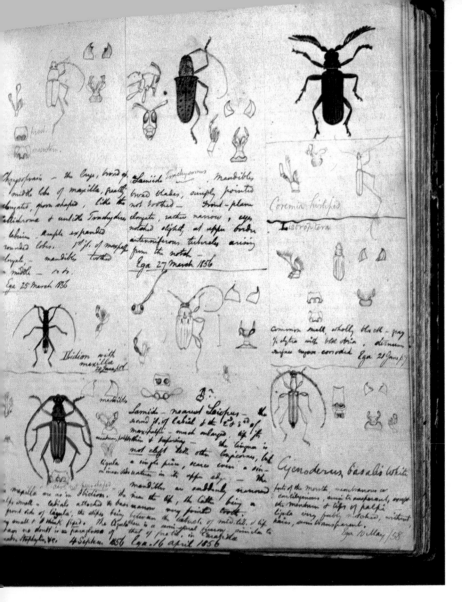

Above: a page from Bates's notebook. He kept careful records of his discoveries, showing here written descriptions of insects he had found, accompanied by drawings of particular parts and a full-scale color drawing of the insect.

There he spent nine years living among primitive tribes and collecting data about the country's wildlife.

Although Wallace's experiences in South America were more exciting than Bates's, his book about them did not do at all well. Only 750 copies of it sold in an 8-year period. Wallace is probably best remembered for being the runner-up in reaching one of the greatest scientific discoveries of all time. When Darwin was finishing his book *The Origin of Species*, Wallace was reaching the same conclusions in the jungles of New Guinea. He wrote a paper about his theory of evolution and natural selection and sent it to Darwin. The older naturalist was tremendously impressed. He later insisted that Wallace's theories should be announced to the scientific community concurrently with his own.

Wallace did not achieve the fame that Darwin did. But his work on natural selection and on the geographical distribution of animals gained him world renown and the respect of the scientific com-

munity. Although he did not fully recover from the fever contracted in South America, Wallace continued to do productive work until his death at the age of 90.

As Wallace was sailing for the Far East, Bates and Spruce continued to scour the Amazon Basin for new wildlife and vegetation. Bates remained on the upper Amazon, above the Negro River, for $4\frac{1}{2}$ years. His base was the village of Ega. "I had a dry and spacious cottage [there], the principal room of which was made a workshop and study. . . . Cages for drying specimens were suspended from the rafters by cords, well anointed, to prevent ants from ascending. . . . My cottage was whitewashed inside and out . . . the floor was of earth; the ventilation was perfect, for the outside air and sometimes the rain as well, entered freely through gaps at the top of the walls under the eaves. . . ."

Bates was appalled at the number of Indians who died from fever. On one occasion he took a small Indian girl into his home to try to

Above: Bates settled contentedly in a village on the upper Amazon, above the Negro River, and remained there for over four years. His life there was full of adventure—here, capturing a crocodile—but he carried on collecting.

cure her. "We took the greatest care of our little patient; had the best nurses in town . . . gave her quinine and the most nourishing food; but it was all of no avail: she sank rapidly. Her liver was enormously swollen and almost as hard to the touch as stone . . . [yet] she was always smiling and full of talk. . . . Scores of helpless children like our poor Oria die at Ega, or on the road, but generally not the slightest care is taken of them during their illness."

During an excursion to the Solimoes River, a westward tributary of the Amazon, Bates saw a turtle oil harvest like the one that had

Left: a drawing by Bates of a bird-killing spider that attacked finches. He included many of his drawings in his book, *Naturalist on the River Amazons,* which was published in 1863.

Right: drawings by Bates of some of the thousands of insects he observed, each meticulously painted in color and carefully numbered in sequence.

fascinated Von Humboldt. Bates wrote of his fear that the practice would lead to the extinction of the animals. "The total number of eggs annually destroyed amounts . . . to 48 million," he wrote, "as each turtle lays about 100, it follows that the yearly offspring of 400,000 turtles is thus annihilated."

Before he left Ega, Bates cataloged some of the most fascinating animals Europe had ever heard of. He described the scarlet-faced monkeys and the moplike Parauacus. He wrote of marmosets and kinkajous, and of 16 species of bats—including the largest of the vampires, which measured $2\frac{1}{2}$ feet across at the wings. He noted the curl-crested toucan, whose feathers look like "thin, horny plates" and whose crest is "arranged on the crown in the form of a wig." The naturalist was intrigued by animals that mimicked each other in markings and coloring. He saw moths that were nearly identical to hummingbirds, and butterflies of entirely different species that were outwardly the same. Bates discovered more than 7,000 species of insects around Ega. He was particularly impressed by the "army" ants that traveled in columns of thousands. "Wherever they move, the whole animal world is set in commotion, and every creature tries to get out of their way."

Bates planned to go 600 miles farther up the Amazon to the foothills of the Andes. But disease again interfered with his plans. In February, 1859, after a bout of the same "ague" of the liver that had killed the Indian girl, Bates returned reluctantly to the coast.

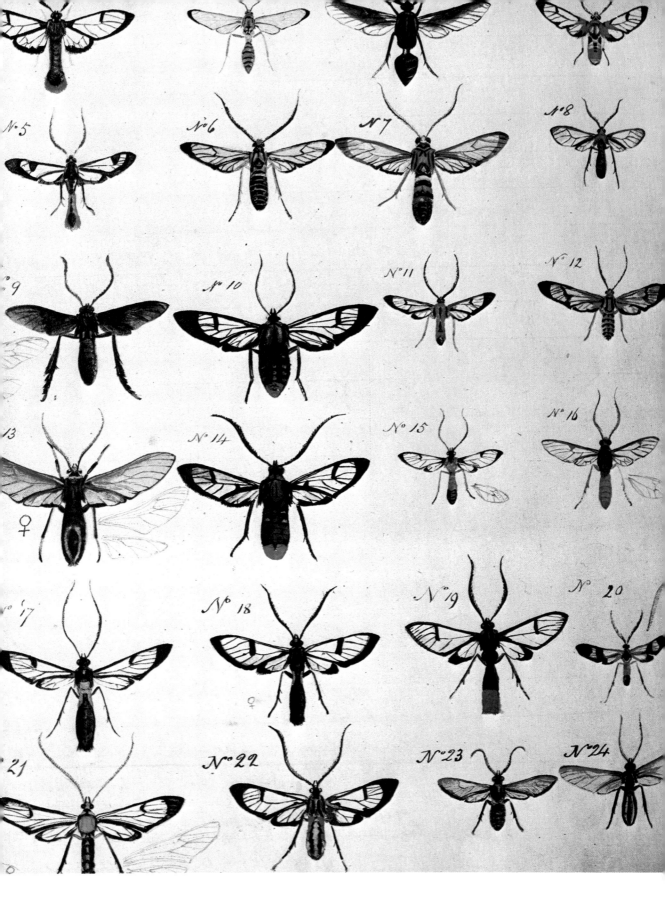

He was amazed at the changes that had taken place in his absence. "I arrived at Pará on the 17th of March after an absence in the interior of seven years and a half," Bates wrote at the end of his book. "My old friends . . . scarcely knew me again . . . and I found Pará greatly changed and improved."

The town had been a sleepy village 11 years before. Now it was becoming a modern metropolis. "Streets, formerly unpaved or strewn with loose stones and sand, were now laid with concrete in a most complete manner . . . the large swamp squares had been drained, weeded, and planted . . . they were now a great ornament . . . instead of an eyesore."

But the city was paying a price for modernization. The cost of living had soared. Bates told how "House rent was most exorbitant; a miserable little place of two rooms, without fixtures or conveniences of any kind, having simply blank walls, cost at the rate of

THE

NATURALIST ON THE RIVER AMAZONS,

A RECORD OF ADVENTURES, HABITS OF ANIMALS, SKETCHES OF
BRAZILIAN AND INDIAN LIFE, AND ASPECTS OF NATURE UNDER
THE EQUATOR, DURING ELEVEN YEARS OF TRAVEL.

By HENRY WALTER BATES.

Saüba Ant.—Female.

IN TWO VOLUMES.—VOL. I.

LONDON:
JOHN MURRAY, ALBEMARLE STREET.
1863.
[The Right of Translation is Reserved.]

Above: the title page from Bates's
book *Naturalist on the River Amazons.*

Left: living in the upper Amazon village,
Bates became familiar with the round
of yearly ceremonials. This drawing
shows a masked dance and wedding
feast celebrated by Tucúna Indians.

£18 a year [then about $54] . . . the hire of servants was beyond the
means of all persons of moderate circumstances; a lazy cook or
porter could not be had for less than three or four shillings a day
beside his board and what he could steal."

What had happened to Pará was also happening to the rest of
Brazil. The reason was rubber. When Richard Spruce came out of
the jungles into Manaus in 1855, he could hardly believe his eyes.
The formerly small river port had become a boom town and center of
the world rubber trade. The population had quadrupled and people
made fortunes overnight. Peasants and shopkeepers ate caviar and
drank champagne. An opera house was under construction, and the
streets of the city were being paved.

During the 35 years that followed, Manaus absorbed almost $50
million in investments. Electric cable cars ran along the streets, and
huge oceangoing ships anchored at her docks. But by 1915, the

boom was over. Henry Wickham's removal of the rubber seeds in 1876 had ended Brazil's monopoly. Manaus became a ghost town.

Bates returned to England, where he met Darwin and was encouraged to write the successful *Naturalist on the River Amazons,* which made him famous. A decade later, Bates was able to incorporate his observations on the mimicry of insects into Darwin's theory of evolution. "The principle," he wrote, "can be none other than natural selection."

Bates died in 1892, at the age of 67. He left behind him a South American collection of 14,712 species of animals. Eight thousand of them were new to science.

Bates's 11-year stay in South America had been scientifically fruitful but relatively unadventurous. Spruce's 13 years there were much more eventful. He found himself continually immersed in danger and intrigue. On a visit to Venezuela in 1853, Spruce forestalled an attack by hundreds of drunken Indians. He stood in the doorway of his house for hours, with a pistol and rifle cocked and ready, before they went away. Later, on the Orinoco, he almost died after a 38-day attack of malaria. Then, as he was gradually recovering, he came near to death at the hands of the four Indian guides who were taking him back downriver. Only Spruce's knowledge of their language saved him. He overheard their murderous plot. When they came for

Above: the Amazon jungle, with, in the foreground, an Indian using a blowpipe to shoot a small animal. Bates used the cumulative total of his experience in the jungle to develop his theory about animals that mimicked other animals in their markings and coloring. Later, his observations were incorporated into Darwin's theories.

Left: Manaus in 1880, when the town was booming. The European demand for rubber turned a sleepy river port into a rushing metropolis where fortunes were being made overnight. When Spruce came out of the jungle into Manaus after an absence of years, he could hardly recognize the town.

him Spruce was sitting up ready with his rifle across his knees.

Heading toward the Andes in 1855, Spruce acquired a partner to help carry his collecting cases—an unemployed sailor named Charlie Nelson. Spruce did not know it, but Nelson was suffering from a mental illness that manifested itself in quick, violent tempers. He had already served a prison sentence in Peru for murder. Soon Spruce's new assistant began to mistreat the Indian guides, kicking and beating them mercilessly. Nelson frequently got into street fights and once beat up a Spanish priest with an ax-handle. When Spruce first tried to get rid of him, Nelson directed his violence at the naturalist. For weeks, Spruce had to sleep with a pistol under his pillow for protection. Finally Nelson agreed to leave, stipulating that he be paid three weeks' wages. Spruce paid up, but Nelson did not survive to spend the money. On his way down the Amazon, Nelson was attacked by Indians and died from his wounds.

Spruce spent two years at Tarapoto, Peru. He was just about to

leave for Ecuador when he was again forced to defend his hut against attack. This time revolutionary soldiers wanted to confiscate his collection. Spruce again stood in his door, gun to his shoulder, and refused to let them enter. After much shouting, they left without firing a shot.

As his little party canoed down the Huallaga River, to its junction with the Marañón, at the start of the journey to Ecuador, the botanist had to navigate rapids and whirlpools. The experiences were frightening for both man and animals, and Spruce's dog went mad. He was forced to shoot the animal, which had traveled with him for years. Just outside Canelos, in view of the Cotopaxi volcano, Spruce ran into a group of headhunters of the Jivaros tribe on a jungle path. Although they could have communicated anyway, since the naturalist was able to speak the native tongue of the Jivaros, Spruce was delighted to discover that they spoke fluent Spanish. And they were not at all interested in collecting his head. Spruce later spent an evening with the headhunters at their camp. There he learned that they hunted only the heads-of enemies suspected of possessing demons—much as the American Pilgrims hanged suspected witches.

When he arrived in Ecuador, Spruce went in search of a man who could sell him cinchona seedlings. He found himself dealing with a doctor called Francisco Nyera, who was a grandson of the man who had killed Seniergues, the French physician in La Condamine's expedition. Spruce eventually succeeded in purchasing some young trees. As he was packing them aboard a river boat for eventual shipment to India, history once again intruded. Church bells started to toll, and a guide brought word that Baron von Humboldt had died thousands of miles away in Berlin.

Three years later, Spruce was forced by ill health to return to England. Plagued by persistent attacks of fever, he had found himself unable to attempt the vigorous climbing and walking he wanted to do. He brought 30,000 plant specimens back to Kew Gardens—many of them previously unknown.

Spruce's material rewards for 13 years of labor were slight. Although his old friend, Wallace, helped him to compile a journal, Spruce could not get it published. Before his death in 1893, Spruce lived out the rest of his life on a paltry yearly pension. Of the hundreds of new plants he discovered, only one bears his name— the moss Sprucea.

Above: a drawing by Spruce of the bark, leaves, and flowers of the cinchona tree. The drug quinine is obtained from the bark.

Right: tapping a wild rubber tree today at Manaus in Brazil. Although the highly profitable industry died when Henry Wickham broke the Brazilian monopoly by transporting seeds out of South America, the trade was continued by a few Brazilians.

Below: rubber manufacture on the banks of the Madeira. The European demand for the new substance created a boom industry that collapsed when it no longer held a monopoly on the plants.

The River of Doubt

8

Above: Theodore Roosevelt, with his hand on the globe, discussing United States policy toward South America. Having led the famous San Juan Hill charge in the Spanish-American War, Roosevelt remained interested in the development and possibilities for exploration in the countries south of the United States, and after his presidential terms he went to Brazil to explore what was then known as the Duvido River, the river of doubt. Left: Roosevelt and his wife sitting surrounded by their children. Teddy Roosevelt was a vigorous, athletic man who thoroughly enjoyed family life.

Deep in the Brazilian highlands, at the western edge of the Mato Grosso, the great forest lands in western Brazil, there flows a wild jungle river that was once known as the Rio Duvido—the river of doubt. The river is more than 950 miles long from source to mouth. For much of its length it is 500 feet wide. Along its winding course the river descends from 500 feet, narrowing dozens of times into steep, rocky gorges that make continuous navigation impossible.

The Duvido is the largest tributary of the Madeira River. In its turn the Madeira is the largest branch of the mighty Amazon. Before 1914, the Duvido was not found on any maps of South America. The best available British map of Brazil showed only a nameless dotted line near where the mouth feeds into the Madeira. In 1909, the unknown river's source in the highlands had been noted and named the Duvido. It was then discovered by a group of explorers who were unable to guess in what direction it flowed or where it ended—hence its name.

Today the river appears on maps as the western branch of the Aripuanã. Its name has changed. Locally, it is known as the Rio Teodoro. To the rest of the world, it is the Roosevelt River.

The exploration of the Duvido River was the last great adventure in the life of a man who had done almost everything else. A celebrated outdoorsman, Theodore Roosevelt, ex-President of the United States, had climbed dozens of mountains from the Adirondacks in New York state to Vesuvius on the Bay of Naples in Italy. He had hunted big game in Africa, lived the hard life of a North Dakota cowboy, and marched with army engineers along the route of the Panama Canal, built during one of his terms as president. In Washington, Roosevelt had involved himself and his staff in strenuous cross-country hikes. On one occasion he infuriated his joint chiefs of staff by sending all Washington-based military officers on a 100-mile hike "to get them back in shape."

When Roosevelt tackled the River of Doubt, he was 54 years old and five years out of his two-term presidency. On the South American expedition, he was accompanied by his son Kermit, a naturalist named George K. Cherrie, and Colonel Candido Rondon, the head of Indian Affairs in Brazil. There were also several junior Brazilian army officers, a few dozen Indian paddlers, and a doctor.

Kermit had accompanied his father on the trip to Africa. He had also done a good deal of mountain climbing and exploring on his

own. Cherrie was a seasoned explorer with some 30 years of jungle experience behind him. Rondon, a Brazilian, was of Indian ancestry. He had spent years exploring the highlands through which they would travel. Years before, he had almost lost his life on an expedition to lay telegraph lines through the wilderness of the Mato Grosso. Before he died, he put 15 new rivers on the map. As a result of his pioneering work, the region that includes the western highlands of Brazil is now called Rondonia.

For Theodore Roosevelt, this was the first prolonged expedition into unexplored territory. His excitement is reflected in the book he wrote about the expedition, *Through the Brazilian Jungles*.

"We were ... on a river which was not merely unknown but unguessed at, no geographer having ever expected its existence,"

Roosevelt wrote. "The river flowed northward toward the equator, but whither it would go, whither it would turn one way or another, the length of its course, where it would come out, the character of the stream itself, and the character of the dwellers along its banks— all these things were yet to be discovered."

On February 27, 1914, after traveling up the Paraguay River and across the highlands, the party started down the Duvido River. Their transport consisted of seven dugout canoes. "One was small, one was cranky, and two were old, waterlogged, and leaky. The other three were good."

Kermit, Rondon, and an army lieutenant named Lyra, were to do the actual surveying. This was a difficult task on the tortuous river, because they had to land and set up the surveying instruments

Above: an Indian dugout canoe moving down the Amazon at sunset. When the Roosevelt party traveled on the river they used seven of these dugout canoes.

dozens of times a day. Theodore Roosevelt's canoe went on ahead to scout out the territory.

When they set out, the rainy season had already begun. The river was overflowing its banks. For the first four days, the canoes made excellent time in the swift current, averaging 20 miles a day. But their initial progress was deceptive. On the fifth day out, they heard the roar of rapids ahead.

"There were many curls and one or two regular falls . . . and they stretched for at least a mile," Roosevelt wrote. "It seemed extraordinary, almost impossible, that so broad a river could in so short a time contract its dimensions to the width of the strangled channel through which it now poured its entire volume. . . ."

The group did not know it, but they were facing only the first of many difficult *portages* (carrying of boats overland from one stretch of water to another). These slowed their progress and exposed them to the many hazards of the surrounding jungle. Insects, while not bothersome in midriver, were fierce on the shore. There were small, stingless bees that swarmed across the men's skins, drinking in the perspiration. There were huge horseflies "the size of bumblebees." There were piume and boroshada flies, whose bites left black, painful sores that lasted for weeks. The men's faces soon became discolored and swollen from the bites. In order to write, Roosevelt wore heavy gloves and a special hat shrouded with netting. Often other insects, such as termites and ants, would eat through the mosquito netting, through the party's stored clothing, and through the supplies.

A portage through untracked jungle proved to be a tedious, backbreaking process. "Dragging the heavy dugouts was labor. . . . All the men were employed at it except the cook and one man who was down with fever," Roosevelt wrote. "A road was chopped through the forest and a couple of hundred stout six-foot poles or small logs were cut as rollers and placed about two yards apart. With block and

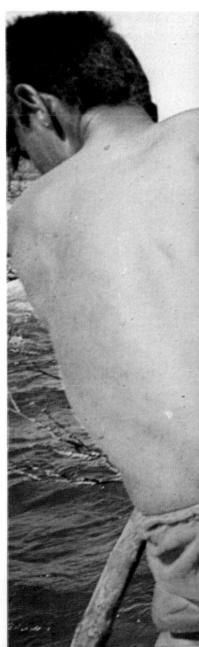

tackle the seven dugouts were hoisted out of the river and up the steep banks until the level was reached . . . then the men harnessed themselves two by two on the drag-rope, which one of their number pried behind with a lever, and the canoe, bumping and sliding, was twitched through the woods."

The first portage was along the Navaite Rapids, named after an Indian subtribe that lived in the area. The trek took 2½ days of constant effort. One of the waterlogged canoes sank just as they were starting and had to be raised. Another canoe was cracked down the middle and had to be patched. This portage, Roosevelt was to learn, was far from being unusually difficult. Two days later,

Left: Indians helping a canoe through some rapids around 1900. The problem was to have at least one man in the canoe while others in the water tried to drag and guide it between the treacherous rocks and shallows.

Below: the difficulties of canoeing in "white water" are much the same in modern times, and the rapids are as dangerous as ever. Amazon travel is still a slow process of battling with the river and portaging through the jungle.

the party again heard the ominous roar of white water. They spent three more days in dragging the canoes along the shore past the rapids.

They were now in territory completely unexplored by any white man. No one knew how far they would have to travel to reach a settlement. To supplement their meager diet, the cook prepared what natural food they could find. They ate palm hearts and wild honey and drank the sticky white liquid of the cow tree that Von Humboldt had sampled on the Venezuelan savannas. For meat, the explorers shot tapirs, parrots, toucans, and monkeys.

By March 10, 1914, the party had traveled only 63 miles. They had portaged past half a dozen rapids and descended nearly 300 feet in the process. Two more of their canoes had been lost, torn from their moorings by the rising water. Later, finding shattered pieces of the dugouts below the rapids, the expedition named that particular stretch of the river "Broken Canoe Rapids."

With the surviving canoes dangerously overloaded, the men were

Right: a brilliantly-colored toucan, *Ranphastos Toco*, one of the kinds of birds that the Roosevelt party hunted to supplement expedition supplies.

Left: a portage of heavy dugout canoes through the jungle when the river had become totally impassable. Roosevelt's party, traveling in the rainy season, slipped and slid along the muddy tracks, tormented by the insects.

forced to stop for several days to build new river craft. The physical discomforts of the trip were increasing. "All of us suffered more or less, our faces and hands swelling," Roosevelt wrote. "Because of the rain and the heat, our clothes were usually wet when we took them off at night and just as wet when we put them on again in the morning."

On March 14, after loading up the two new boats, the expedition set out on the river once again. "Our heavily laden, clumsy dugouts were sunk to within three or four inches of the surface of the river," said Roosevelt.

Nevertheless, when the group encountered yet another series of rapids, they decided to ride them out to save time. "Our progress had been so very slow that unless we made up the time it was probable that we would be short of food before we got where we could expect to procure any more."

Pushing ahead, the party steered the dugouts through a torrent of whirlpools and foaming water. "The two biggest rapids we only just made," wrote Roosevelt, "and after each we had hastily to push ashore in order to bail. In one set of big ripples or waves my canoe was nearly swamped."

Then the expedition drifted into tragedy. Rounding a bend in the river the party encountered one of the worst stretches of white water they had yet seen. Kermit Roosevelt paddled on ahead with two Indian helpers, Simplicio and Joao, to survey the extent of the rapids. But as the three were returning to the main bank, their dugout was sucked into the swift current. Roosevelt watched helplessly as his son and his companions were swept away.

"One of the shifting whirlpools . . . came downstream, whirled them around, and swept them so close to the rapids that no human power could avoid going over them . . . the water came aboard, wave after wave, as they raced down. They reached the bottom with the canoe upright, but so full as barely to float. The paddlers urged her toward the shore. They had nearly reached the bank when another whirlpool or whirling eddy tore them away and hurried them back to midstream, where the dugout filled and turned over. Poor Simplicio must have been pulled under at once, and his life beaten

Left: shooting through white water shallows of the Upper Amazon. The front man on the raft is trying to maintain some control of the craft hurtling through the water by using his paddle.

out on the boulders beneath the racing torrent. He never rose again. Kermit clutched his rifle and climbed back on the bottom of the upset boat. In a minute he was swept into the second series of rapids and whirled away from the rolling boat, losing his rifle. The water beat his helmet down over his head and face. He was dragged beneath the surface, and when he rose at last he was almost drowned. . . . He was in a swift but quiet water and swam toward an overhanging branch. His jacket hindered him, but he knew he was too nearly gone to be able to get it off . . . he realised that the utmost his failing strength could do was to reach the branch. He reached, and clutched it, and then almost lacked strength to haul himself out on the land . . . it was a very narrow escape.''

Above: Theodore Roosevelt's group on the East African expedition in 1909, when his son Kermit had also been one of the party. From the left they are R. J. Cuninghame, Kermit, Roosevelt, Edmund Heller, and Hugh H. Heatley.

Before going on, the men erected a memorial to the dead man. It read, "Here lies poor Simplicio."

"On an expedition such as ours," Roosevelt pointed out, "death is one of the accidents that may at any time occur and narrow escapes . . . are too common to be felt as they would be elsewhere. One mourns sincerely, but mourning cannot interfere with labor."

The expedition was now traveling through the land of the savage Nhambiquara Indians who had probably never seen a white man before. The explorers had seen Indian signs and come across several abandoned settlements during their first month of travel. Now they had a more ominous indication of the Indians' presence. As they were portaging yet another set of rapids only a few miles beyond those in which Kermit had nearly died, the explorers heard strange howling in the woods nearby. One of the three dogs ran toward the sound and out of sight. A few seconds later there was a yelp of sudden pain, then silence. Walking into the forest, the explorers came across the dog's body. It had two arrows protruding from its side.

Below: sweeping down the rapids on the Amazon. As the rushing water hurtles the canoe along, its occupants fight for control, struggling to keep away from the dangerous rocks.

Rather than camp in hostile territory, the party decided to lower the canoes over the rapids. Leaving beads and other gifts near the dead animal as a sign of goodwill, the men hastily devised a system of pulleys and began feeding the canoes into the frothing stream. The last canoe over the cliff was the new dugout. It had nearly reached the bottom when the rope holding it snagged on a protruding rock. The swinging motion of the craft drew the rope slowly back and forth against the sharp surface. The men watched, frustrated, as the rope frayed and finally snapped. The new boat, which had taken three days to build, sank forever beneath the foaming water.

On March 19, the expedition stopped again to construct new canoes. The group had now been traveling for almost three weeks, yet they had covered barely 70 miles. As Roosevelt noted, the river was so winding "that we had gone two miles for every one we made northward." The explorer estimated that they had three or four times the distance so far traveled still to go. Their food was already half gone. By now some of the Indian paddlers were barely able to

Below: three Indian girls with brilliantly-colored necklaces. The Roosevelt party brought beads and other small gifts for the Indians they would encounter along the river. One little collection of gifts was left for the unseen Indians who had killed one of the dogs, to show them that the expedition members meant no harm.

walk on their swollen feet. Several were suffering from fever.

The members of the party were down to two meals a day. "It was only on the rare occasions when we had killed some monkeys or curassows [large gamebirds found in Central and South America], or caught some fish, that everybody had enough to eat." Despite his increasing physical discomfort, Roosevelt still found it possible to enjoy the scenery. "Ahead of us the shrouded river stretched between dim walls of forest, half seen in the mist," he wrote one morning. "The sun burned up the fog and loomed through it in a

Right: Roosevelt with Candido Rondon, the head of Indian Affairs in Brazil, deep in the interior of the Amazon after an obviously successful hunt.

red splendor that changed first to gold and then to white . . . this camp was very lovely. It was on the edge of a bay, into which the river broadened immediately below the rapids. There was a beach of white sand, where we bathed and washed our clothes. All around us, and across the bay, and on both sides of the long water street made by the river, rose the splendid forest."

Apart from the rapids, there was the ever-present danger of piranhas. The explorers spotted several in nearly every pool along the river. Earlier in the journey a piranha had devoured the tail of

Left: a piranha fish on the hook. The constant presence of the deadly flesh-eaters made washing and bathing dangerous pastimes. Years before, Rondon had had his foot partially eaten by piranhas on another jungle river.

one of the dogs. Years before Rondon had had part of his foot
eaten away by one of these cannibal fish on a similar jungle river.
Roosevelt noted that the temperament of the piranhas seemed to vary
with the locale. Bathing and laundering were always a risky business.

At one point, as they paused to portage some more rapids, the
men supplemented a sparse meal of toucan and toasted Brazil nuts
with the flesh of a large piranha. Roosevelt said it was very good
eating.

Next day, the group was portaging a rocky gorge when they came
upon some strange symbols carved in the rock. They were of a type
that even the Indian expert Rondon had never seen before. "The

signs consisted, upon the upper flat part of the rock, of four multiple circles with a dot in the middle, very accurately made and about a foot and a half in diameter; and below them, on the side of the rock, four multiple M's or inverted W's. What these curious symbols represented, or who made them, we could not of course form the slightest idea. The meaning and origin of these symbols have remained a mystery."

The explorers were now hoping that the worst of the rapids were behind them. But they were not to be so fortunate. On March 28, the terrain around them changed abruptly. Before, they had been in a plateau region. Now they were entering a mountainous area.

Above: one of the vast waterfalls on the Amazon. Sudden drops in the level of the rivers are recurring features of the South American terrain.

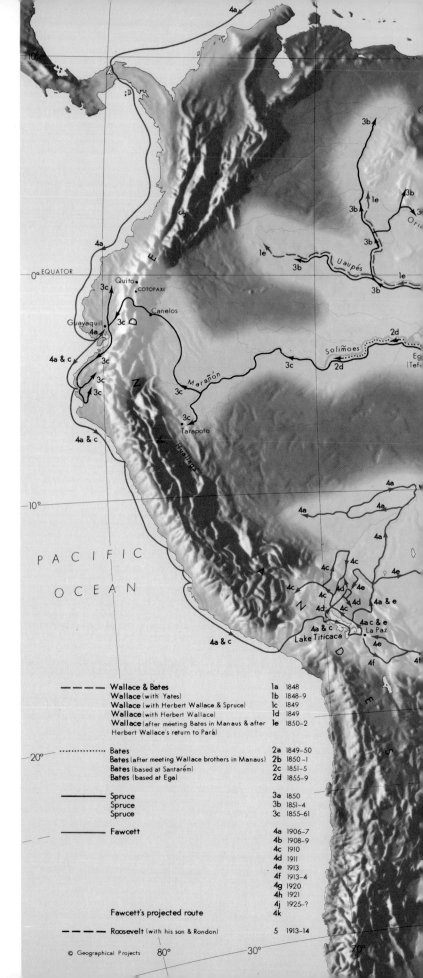

Right: northern South America, showing the routes of British and American explorers in the period 1848-1925. The last of these—the Englishman Percy Fawcett—disappeared without trace in the western Mato Grosso in 1925. The map shows the route he planned to follow and the last point he is known to have reached.

	Wallace & Bates	1a	1848
	Wallace (with Yates)	1b	1848-9
	Wallace (with Herbert Wallace & Spruce)	1c	1849
	Wallace (with Herbert Wallace)	1d	1849
	Wallace (after meeting Bates in Manaus & after Herbert Wallace's return to Pará)	1e	1850-2
	Bates	2a	1849-50
	Bates (after meeting Wallace brothers in Manaus)	2b	1850-1
	Bates (based at Santarém)	2c	1851-5
	Bates (based at Ega)	2d	1855-9
	Spruce	3a	1850
	Spruce	3b	1851-4
	Spruce	3c	1855-61
	Fawcett	4a	1906-7
		4b	1908-9
		4c	1910
		4d	1911
		4e	1913
		4f	1913-4
		4g	1920
		4h	1921
		4j	1925-?
	Fawcett's projected route	4k	
	Roosevelt (with his son & Rondon)	5	1913-14

© Geographical Projects

ATLANTIC

OCEAN

EQUATOR 0°

Mouths of the Amazon
1b
1a

I. DE MARAJÓ
Pará (Belém)
1c
2a & c
1a & 1c

Amazon
5
2a & c
1a

Manaus
1d
1c
Santarém
1e
1d
2a & d
3a
Xingú
Tocantins
3c
3a
Madeira
2c
Tapajós
2c
Aripuanã
2c

Theodore Roosevelt
5
Araguaia
4j?
4k
4k
10°

Dead Horse Camp
4k

ONIA
4f
4g & j
4j
4b & f
Planalto
4h
Salvador
4f
4b
do Mato
4h
4b & f
4b
4g & j
4h
4h
4f
4b
4b
Grosso
4b,g & j
5
5
BRAZILIAN HIGHLANDS

4b
4g & j
Paraná
5
20°

Paraguay
Rio de Janeiro
4g & j

TROPIC OF CAPRICORN

Paraná
Uruguay
5

5 to Montevideo
60°
50°
40°
30°
30°

0 100 200 300 400 500
Miles

Roosevelt compared it in appearance to the Allegheny Mountains at home. Ahead of the party was an impenetrable gorge that extended for almost three miles in length. It was broken only by a series of steep waterfalls, one of them 35 feet high.

The rocky landscape made portage of the canoes impossible. The group had to decide whether to abandon them altogether or to lower them over the multiple falls. Not knowing how many miles of jungle still lay before them, they decided on the latter course. Stripping themselves of all but essentials, the men spent three days laboriously lowering the canoes through the gorge. Standing waist deep in the foaming water, on slippery boulders, they braced themselves perilously on the edges of the falls. Slowly they fed the ropes downward. The walls of the gorge were so sheer that at the worst places they had to cling to narrow shelves on the face of the rock, while letting the canoes down with ropes.

Five canoes were finally through. The bottom was knocked out of the sixth and it had to be abandoned. "We had been exactly a month going down an uninterrupted succession of rapids," Roose-

Above: a group photograph of guides and servants on an Amazon expedition in the 1890's. The explorers of that period found that the men willing to go into the jungles with them were often half-breed drifters, very tough men who were not always entirely trustworthy deep in the interior.

Right: a giant fish caught in the Amazon by a group traveling in the 1870's. This fish is called the Pira-Ruca *(Sudis gigas).* Roosevelt's group caught a giant catfish that had a half-digested monkey in its stomach.

velt wrote, "during that month . . . we had lost four of the canoes with which we started, and one other, which we had built; and the life of one man; and the life of a dog which by its death had in all probability saved the life of Colonel Rondon."

Roosevelt estimated that they had traveled about 120 miles up to this point. Less than a quarter of that distance, he thought, had been spent going due north toward the Amazon. They had averaged only $1\frac{1}{4}$ miles a day. Meanwhile they had descended nearly 480 feet.

Three days later, as the group struggled through still another portage, a gunshot was heard in the woods. One of the Indian paddlers had gone berserk and killed the overseer. The other men found his body lying by the forest path. He lay in a huddle in a pool of his own blood, where he had fallen, shot through the heart. Finding the gun, Roosevelt and Rondon decided that there was no purpose in pursuing the murderer who had escaped into the jungle. Had they caught him, they reasoned, they would have had to keep him under constant guard for the rest of the journey. It would have been an almost impossible task in view of the weakened condition of the men. Alone, the murderer's fate was certain death.

Hunger, overwork, and constant exposure were now beginning to tell on the remaining members of the expedition. Insect bites that had been irritating before now became dangerously abscessed. Kermit Roosevelt went down with fever and had to stop working for several days. Roosevelt himself stumbled and hurt his leg badly. As he was recuperating, he too contracted the fever. Despite daily doses of quinine the fever was spreading. Lieutenant Lyra and the naturalist Cherrie both had severe dysentery. The men's clothes were in rags and their shoes had rotted away. The future of the expedition seemed dark.

Then on April 6, the land abruptly leveled off. Pushed by the

still-strong current, the party made a record 30 miles in a day. Their spirits were further buoyed when one of the men caught a giant catfish nearly four feet long. As the men were cleaning it, they were astonished to find the remains of a monkey in its stomach. Roosevelt reported being told of even larger catfish that inhabit the Amazon and prey on men.

The respite was short-lived. From April 8 to April 14, the explorers portaged a continuous succession of rapids. By April 15, half the crew were too sick to work. Roosevelt's fever returned and his bruised leg became abscessed. The doctor had to install a drain into the swollen limb, and Roosevelt's temperature soared to 105°F. He was nearly unable to walk. Roosevelt told his companions that if his condition did not improve, he was to be left behind. "Fortunately," he wrote in his book, "I was put to no such test . . . we had passed the last of the rapids of the chasms. When my serious troubles came, we had only canoe riding ahead of us."

On the morning of April 16, an excited paddler began yelling and pointing at the river bank. There, in a clearing, was a new, palm-thatched hut. They had reached the uppermost outpost of the rubber workers. Survival was assured. The exhausted, near-naked explorers spent their first night under a roof in nearly two months.

For the next few days, the canoes drifted past dozens of similar houses. Roosevelt was amazed to find an "unknown" river so populated. "It was astonishing before, when we were on a river about the size of the upper Rhine or Elbe to realize that no geographer had any idea of its existence. . . . But, here . . . was a river with people dwelling along the banks, some of whom had lived in the neighborhood for 8 or 10 years; and yet on no standard map was there a hint of the river's existence . . . the place actually occupied by it was filled, on the maps, by other imaginary streams or by mountain ranges."

Fifteen days after sighting the first rubber plantation, the expedition triumphantly reached the Amazon city of Manaus. They had traveled from the source to the mouth of the river. For most of the last two weeks, Roosevelt had had a raging fever. He lay flat on his back at the bottom of a canoe shielded from the sun by only a flimsy piece of cloth.

He never regretted the effort. The surveying had gone on throughout all their privations and struggles. "We had now put on the map a river . . . [625 miles] of which the existence was not merely unknown but impossible if the standard maps were correct."

Roosevelt never entirely recovered from the fever. Although he continued to hike, swim, and ride at his estate, the exploration of the Duvido River was his last great adventure. He died five years after his return, on January 6, 1919.

When his son Quentin was killed in action in France in 1918, Roosevelt had written: "Only those are fit to live who do not fear to die; and none are fit to die who have shrunk from the joy of life. Both life and death are parts of the same great adventure."

Above: a newspaper cartoon showing Teddy Roosevelt in the role of a hunter. His exploits were vividly reported in the popular press. The American people were fascinated by Roosevelt's unquenchable enthusiasm for the adventurous outdoor life.

Left: Roosevelt, big game hunter in Africa. But the Duvido River expedition was his last—he never completely recovered from the fever he had there.

In 1925, a middle-aged Englishman, Colonel Percy Harrison Fawcett, set off into the western Mato Grosso to look for a lost city. Some weeks later, he wrote to his wife from the area where Theodore Roosevelt and his party had observed the indecipherable Indian signs. Then Fawcett disappeared without trace.

Percy Fawcett had been born in England in 1867. He spent more than 20 years as a military surveyor, geographer, and engineer with the British Army. Then he turned to the career he had always wanted for himself—exploration. Fawcett's first job was in South America. He went on a mission to survey the common boundary of Peru, Bolivia, and Brazil for the Royal Geographical Society. The job took four years. When Fawcett re-emerged from the jungle in 1910, he was an expert on how to survive its hazards.

Over the next 15 years, Fawcett made several more exploratory journeys through the almost unknown jungle country south of the Amazon. He traveled extensively among hostile, sometimes cannibal, tribes.

In the course of his wanderings, Fawcett came into possession of a 150-year-old map. The map had been drawn by a man who claimed to have found a lost city deep in the Mato Grosso. It showed a walled town surrounded by jungle in the middle of hundreds of acres of cultivated land. Fawcett named the lost

Left: Colonel Percy Fawcett with his party at the source of the Verde. Fawcett is the taller of the two central figures. His party vanished without trace in the Mato Grosso.

Right: bones exhibited in a Rio de Janeiro anthropological museum as Fawcett's remains. They were found in 1951, in a shallow grave in the jungle.

city "Z." He made up his mind that he would go and search for it.

The colonel's Indian friends supported what the document said. They also told an incredible tale of their own. They told Fawcett of another great river beside which lay the ruins of a large city. The city was built on the shore of a wide lake at the top of a great waterfall. "Before the fall, the river seemed to widen out into a great lake, emptying itself they had no notion where," Fawcett wrote to a friend. "In a quiet water below the fall was a figure of a man carved in white rock (quartz or perhaps rock crystal), which moved to and fro with the force of the current."

On the way to this strange city, said the Indians, was a tall tower from which lights shone every night to frighten trespassers away. The trouble with the stories Fawcett heard was that no one knew exactly where these cities were. The closest the colonel could come to an estimate was that they lay between the São Francisco and Xingú rivers. That meant they could be anywhere in an area of about 1,000 square miles.

Fawcett was not deterred. "Our route will be from Dead Horse Camp," he wrote, "roughly north-west to the Xingú, visiting on the way an ancient stone tower which is the terror of the surrounding Indians, as at night it is lighted from doors and windows. Beyond the Xingú we shall take to the forest to a point midway between that river and the Araguaya."

Financed by the North American Newspaper Alliance (NANA), which bought all rights to the story, Fawcett set out across the Mato Grosso in 1925. His son Jack and a young friend, Raleigh, accompanied him. "We go with eight animals," he wrote to his wife, "three saddle mules, four cargo mules, and a marinha—a leading animal which keeps the others together. . . . Raleigh I am anxious about. He still has one leg in a bandage . . . so far we have plenty of food . . . but I am not sure how long this will last. . . . I cannot hope to stand up to this journey better than Jack or Raleigh, but I had to do it. Years tell, in spite of the spirit of enthusiasm." It was the last letter Fawcett ever wrote. Nothing more was heard from him. In 1928, NANA organized a search party to go into the Mato Grosso in search of Fawcett or his remains. Then, in 1930, a journalist named Albert de Winton died searching for him. But no trace was found of the three men or the Indian bearers who went with them.

Even nowadays, there are still rumors from time to time about aging white men who live deep in the jungle with Indian tribes. Fawcett, of course, would be long dead. But could Jack Fawcett or Raleigh still be alive?

Considering the hazards of the jungles—the insects, the jaguars and peccaries, the man-eating piranhas in every pond—their survival is unlikely. But perhaps the three men found sanctuary. Perhaps they found the beautiful kingdom they had sought and decided to stay. The jungle keeps the secret.

South America was discovered by Europeans nearly 500 years ago.

Above: Jack Fawcett, Colonel Fawcett's son, and Raleigh Rimell at Dead Horse Camp. It was from here that the men meant to travel northwest to the Xingú, and from there into the forest. In Fawcett's last letter to his wife, he mentioned that he was already concerned about Rimell who had injured his leg and was still in bandages. Below: a drawing by Fawcett's younger son, Brian, of an attack by piranhas.

Right: a photograph taken by Brian
Fawcett of the grave in which the bones
were found by Orlando Villas Boas in
1951. Investigations in 1952, proved
that the bones belonged to no member
of the Fawcett party. The mystery
was deepened since the Xingú Indians
—in whose territory the bones were
discovered—never bury their victims.
There is still no answer to the problem
of what became of the party.

Right: a drawing by Frederick Catherwood of the Maya temple at Copan in
Honduras. Catherwood and John Lloyd
Stephens discovered the temple in the
mid-1800's. At first, all they saw
was a flight of stone steps, but when
they hacked away the enveloping jungle
the temple itself was revealed.

Above: remains of a past civilization
lying deep in the Mato Grosso jungle,
almost buried in the lush
vegetation. Frequently such moss- and
creeper-covered ruins are only
visible to the highly-trained eye.

Yet vast areas of the continent still remain unexplored. There are the matted, steaming selvas of the Amazon Basin, the thorny, barely penetrable jungles of the Gran Chaco, the great lowlying plain of Argentina, and the densely forested Mato Grosso of Brazil that stretches for nearly 500,000 square miles.

Archaeologists suspect that all of these unexplored areas contain remnants of ancient societies still awaiting discovery. Some of these societies may have been as great as those already discovered. Peru, for instance, had various highly developed agricultural societies in 2000 B.C. The first hunters and nomads lived in Peru long before, probably as long ago as 8000 B.C.

Over so many centuries, the jungle can camouflage a large city so thoroughly that it will be invisible to all but the highly trained eye. When the Maya kingdom of Tikal was discovered in Central America in 1848, it was so overgrown that even the great pyramids could not be seen from more than a hundred yards away.

In 1911, the American explorer and archaeologist Hiram Bingham stumbled across what may have been the last stronghold of the Inca in the Andes Mountains. Then Bingham discovered the ancient city of Machu Picchu. The city was perched on a mountain top 2,000 feet above one of the most frequently traveled roads in Peru. The jungle had completely covered its steep temple stairways, great plazas, and cone-shaped observatory.

The remains of the Bolivian kingdom of the Tiahuanaco Indians were also found in the 1900's. Its capital was built 12,570 feet above sea level on the shore of Lake Titicaca. The level of the lake has dropped in the 11 centuries since the city flourished, but remnants of its once-spectacular beauty still survive. The entrance to the city is a great arch called the Gateway to the Sun. It is fashioned out of a single giant piece of stone. Carved into the gate is the figure of a god surrounded by warriors. At one time the figures were inlaid with gold. Their eyes are made of semiprecious stones.

In 1943, the archaeologist and naturalist Julio C. Tello discovered ruins of another sacred Indian city, Chavin de Hauntar. Among its ruins is a three-story stone building called the castle. Entirely built of cut, unmortared stone, it dates back to the 700's.

Excavations are still going on in the ruins of the city of San Augustin in Colombia. It nestles between Andean ridges, 4,534 feet above the sea. It was first discovered in 1914.

Above: the gate at Tiahuanaco, Bolivia. The city was originally on the shore of Lake Titicaca, but as the level of the water has dropped it now stands above the lake. The entrance to the city is through this great arch called the Gateway to the Sun.

And at least part of the golden kingdom that eluded Raleigh in the 1500's has been found.

For hundreds of years explorers were intrigued by Indian tales about the gold and jewels that lay at the bottom of a sacred lake named Guatavita, in Colombia. In 1912, the lake was finally drained. The stories proved to have a basis in fact. Millions of dollars worth of precious gems and golden ornaments were found at the bottom. As Raleigh had believed, there was an El Dorado, hundreds of miles up the Orinoco. But it was farther up than anyone had suspected.

There are still unsolved mysteries. Orellana, for instance, spoke of broad highways cut into the jungles of the Amazon basin. Were

these roads part of the kingdom of the Inca before they migrated to the Andes? Or were they the remains of an early Aztec kingdom that had existed before the migration to Mexico? No one has yet discovered.

South America today contains some of the earth's last great frontiers. How many more treasure-filled cities lie under its blankets of jungle moss and tangled vines? Apart from the savannas and pampas, very little of South America can be mapped from the air. A canopy of tropical vegetation shuts the wilderness off from the most modern methods of cartography. Only men on foot, willing to risk death as their predecessors of centuries before had done, will be able to unearth the ancient secrets of the jungle.

Above: another drawing by Catherwood of an ancient temple emerging from the jungle. This one is at Tuloom, in Central America. The jungles of Central and South America are so dense that whole cities can be completely hidden from view. Some have been rediscovered, but no one knows how many may still lie concealed.

Left: Alexander von Humboldt, the great naturalist-explorer who traveled widely in South America early in the 1800's. This caricature shows Von Humboldt loaded with specimens of plants and insects that he found on his journeys. He is also holding a copy of *Cosmos,* the book he never completed.

Appendix

This appendix contains a necessarily very small selection of passages from the wealth of original firsthand material recording the exploits and impressions of travelers in South America. Almost all the earliest explorers of the new continent left some written account of their journeys. Later explorers wrote some of the most popular adventure stories of all time, as well as some of the most valuable scientific records of the flora and fauna of South America, some of them unsurpassed to this day.

The extracts quoted reflect the different experiences and different aims of various travelers. An account of the terrible sufferings of the conquistador Gonzalo Pizarro and his companions on their agonizing return journey to Quito appears first. For most later travelers, there was less physical suffering, but exploration was always a difficult task. A passage by Richard Spruce, the British traveler of the 1800's, shows that 300 years after the first journeys, traveling in unmapped territory could still be an extremely arduous undertaking. Disaster and drama were never far away, as witnessed by Charles Darwin's account of the earthquake in Chile, and by the fact that although Percy Fawcett's letter got back from the jungle, he himself never did. Other more peaceful themes are descriptions of two important natural features of South America, the llama and the rubber tree, and a list of the many skillfully made artifacts of some of the most primitive tribesmen of the Amazon basin.

Capsule biographies for quick and easy reference are included, arranged in alphabetical order, in the second part of the appendix. Maps in the same section show the routes followed by explorers not previously mapped in the book.

The glossary that follows the biographies gives a fuller explanation of terms used in the book and definitions of unusual words and phrases. Index and credit information complete the appendix.

Left: one of the giant trees of the Brazilian jungle. The tangled jungles of South America are one of the last unexplored regions on earth. The many inventions that have made exploration easier are of little use in their matted undergrowth. Only an explorer willing to brave their dangers on foot will be able to find out what secrets they still hide.

Return to Quito

While Orellana was making history by crossing South America,
his leader, Gonzalo Pizarro, was left to make his unhappy way
back to Quito with the remnant of his men. A Spanish writer
of the late 1500's describes Pizarro's experiences.

"Now Gonsalo Pisarro, beyng left succourlesse and voyde of
help for his Nauigation, and the only way to prouide sustenance
for his armie, yet he found somwhat amonge the Indians for barter
of small bels and glasses: notwithstandying his greefe and heauinesse
was not small, wher vpon he determined to returne backe agayne
to Quito, from whence he had trauailed more than 400 leagues of
most euill way, among Mountaynes, and country vnhabited: the
which when he had discouered, hee wondered at his owne trauayles,
which he had passed, and escaped the cruel death of hunger in the
wildernes of Mountaynes, wher 40 of his men ended their daies,
without any hope of succour but euen as they axed for meate,
lening to trees, they fel downe dead with very hunger. But now
committing him self to God hee returned by another way, leauing
the way that he came, which was not only troublesome to passe, but
also voyde of al sustenance, and so . . . sought another way . . . in
which they had much to do to sustaine life.

"In this manner Gonsalo Pisarro continued on his way toward
Quito, where as longe before hee gaue aduice of his returne, where-
upon the Cittizens of Quito prouided great aboundance of hogs,
and sheepe, and came out of the citie to meete him on his way:
they caryed also with them some horses and apparrel, for Gonsalo
Pisarro, and his Captaines, the which succor came vnto him, being
50 leagues from Quito, who comming vnto him with such prouision,
God he knoweth, how ioyfully it was accepted, but cheefely the
victuals: Gonsalo Pisarro and his company, were almost naked, for
long sithence with the great waters of rayne, and otherwise, their
clothes were rotted from their bodies, so that now, each of them
had but only two small Deare skins, which couered their fore parts,
and also their hinder partes: some had lefte olde rotten breeches,
and shooes made of raw deare skins: their swords wanted scabards
and were spoyled with rust they came all on foote, their armes and
legs, were scratched with shrubs and bryers, their iestures seemed
like vnto dead men, so that scarcely their freends and olde acquaintance knew them: In which painefull Iorney, in more then

200 leagues, they could finde no salte, which they found to bee a great want vnto them. But when they were come into the countrey of Quito, and had receaued that freendly succour, they fel on their knees, and kissed the ground, yeeldinge vnto God moste humble and harty thankes, who had deliuered them from so many perrils and daungers."

Conquest of Peru *Augustin de Zarate trans. by Thomas Nicholas (The Penguin Press: London, 1933) pp. 160–162.*

Below: Pizarro's agonizing return to Quito brought him little peace, for he discovered there that his brother, conqueror of Peru, had been killed. In the battles that followed for the control of the Inca lands, Gonzalo was defeated, taken prisoner, and executed.

The Lawless Plains

Here Von Humboldt describes the robber-infested plains of South America. He explains how these immense grasslands act as a barrier to the development of the new continent.

"The llanos [plains] were then infested by an immense number of robbers, who assassinated the whites that fell into their hands with an atrocious refinement of cruelty. Nothing is more deplorable than the administration of justice in the colonies beyond sea. We every where found the prisons filled with malefactors, on whom sentence is not passed till after waiting seven or eight years. Nearly a third of the prisoners succeed in making their escape; and the unpeopled plains, filled with herds, afford them both an asylum and food. . . . The insalubrity of the prisons would be at its height, if they were not emptied from time to time by the flight of the prisoners. It often happens also, that sentences of death . . . cannot be executed for want of a hangman. In these cases a barbarous custom prevails . . . of pardoning one criminal on the condition of his hanging the others . . . .

"If, in the peaceful times when Mr. Bonpland and myself had the good fortune to travel through both Americas, the *llanos* were even then the refuge of malefactors . . . how much worse must this state of things have become in consequence of civil discords, and amid that sanguinary struggle, which has terminated by giving liberty and independence to those vast regions! Our wastes and heaths are but a feeble image of the savannahs of the New Continent which for the space of eight or ten thousand square leagues are smooth as the surface of the sea. The immensity of their extent insures impunity to vagabonds for they are better concealed in the savannahs than in our mountains and forests; and it is easy to conceive, that the artifices of a European police could not be easily put in practice, where there are travellers and no roads, herds and no herdsmen, and farms so solitary, that, notwithstanding the powerful action of the *mirage*, several days' journey may be made without seeing one appear within the horizon."

"In traversing the *llanos* of Caraccas, Barcelona, and Cumana, which succeed each other from west to east, from the snowy mountains of Merida to the Delta of the Oroonoko [Orinoco], we ask ourselves whether these vast tracts of land be destined by Nature to serve eternally for pasture, or [whether] the plough and the space of the labourer will one day subject them to cultivation. This question is

Left: Von Humboldt found the great variety of rock formations fascinating and took careful notes on many. This formation of basaltic rocks, called the cascade of Regla, is in Mexico.

Below: the dragon tree of Oratava, which Von Humboldt saw in Teneriffe in 1799. How it reached Teneriffe from its native home in the East Indies still remains an interesting problem.

... important, as the *llanos,* placed at the two extremities of South America, are obstacles to the political union of the provinces they separate. They prevent the agriculture of the coast of Venezuela from extending toward Guyana, and that of Potosi toward the mouth of the Rio de la Plata.

"In no other part of the world are the configuration of the ground and the state of its burden marked by stronger features; and no where do they act more sensibly [noticeably] on the divisions of the social body, already divided by the original difference of colour, and by individual liberty. It is not in the power of man to change that diversity of climates, which the inequalities of the soil produce on a small space of ground, and which give rise to the antipathy of the inhabitants."

Personal Narrative of Travels to the New Continent *Alexander von Humboldt (Longman, Rees, Orme, Brown, and Green: London, 1826) pp. 56–59.*

The Inconvenience of a New Country

Karl von Martius was a German botanist who explored Brazil in the second decade of the 1800's. At that time Brazil was very much an uncultivated land.

"The mite called *carobatos* is one of the most formidable plagues. These little animals, from the size of a poppy-seed to that of a linseed, live in societies, and crowded by hundreds in the grass and on dry leaves. As soon as the traveler touches such a plant, they very quickly penetrate through his clothes to the skin, where they eat in, particularly in the more tender parts, and cause an intolerable itching, which is increased by the inevitable rubbing, and in the end produces an inflamed blister. The securest remedy immediately to get rid of these teasing enemies is to pick them off from the skin, or if they have not already eaten too far in, to kill them by rubbing with brandy, or with tobacco infused in water, or by fumigating with tobacco over the fire. Only those who have themselves experienced this evil, so common in the torrid zone, can form an idea of the sufferings to which the naturalist, who is constantly in the open air, is exposed. Happily all these inconveniences are of such a nature that they may be greatly diminished, if not

Below: for centuries the rivers were the only routes into the interior of Brazil. Here a group of explorers makes its way into the unknown jungle.

wholly removed, by a knowledge of the country, and the application of approved remedies. With the increasing population and cultivation of the country they will gradually diminish. When the inhabitants have cut down the woods, drained marshes, made roads, everywhere founded villages and towns, and thus by degrees triumphed over the rank vegetation and the noxious animals, all the elements will willingly second, and amply recompense the activity of man. But before Brazil shall have attained this period of civilisation, the uncultivated land may yet prove a grave to thousands of adventurers. Attracted by the constant beauty of the climate, the richness and the fertility of the soil, many leave their native land, to seek another home in a foreign hemisphere, and in a quite different climate. However true the suppositions are on which they found the expectations of a happy result of their enthusiastic enterprise, it is far from realising the hopes of the emigrants, especially those from the north of Europe; and how shall the inhabitant of the temperate zone, suddenly removed as a cultivator of the soil to Rio de Janeiro, or perhaps even to the shores of the Amazons, to a foreign climate, a foreign soil, a new mode of life and subsistence, surrounded by Portuguese, whose language he neither understands, nor easily learns, how shall he be happy and maintain himself in this country? . . . . He, however, who has happily passed over the first trials, who has secured a settlement in the beautiful country of Brazil, and accustomed himself to the tropical climate, will most willingly acknowledge it for his second home; nay, if he has again visited Europe, he will . . . celebrate Brazil as the fairest and most glorious country on the surface of the globe."

Travels in Brazil *J. B. Von Spix and C. F. P. Von Martius (Longman, Hurst, Rees, Orme, Brown & Green: London, 1824) pp. 260–261.*

Below: a musical wood-cricket from Brazil. Not all the insects found in the Brazilian jungles are the pests that Von Martius describes so vividly.

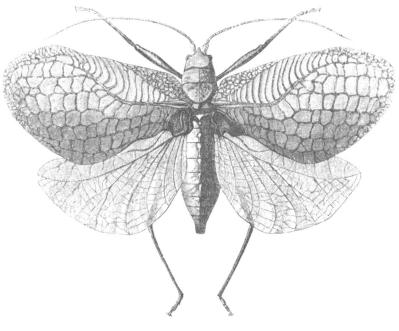

Camels of the New World

Most early explorers of South America used the same beast of burden as the Indians in many places still do—the llama. Here an American naval officer, who traveled widely in South America in the 1850's, describes the llama and the wild vicuña, both members of the camel family.

"Returning from the mine we met a drove of llamas on their way from the hacienda. This is quite an imposing sight, especially when the drove is encountered suddenly at a turn of the road. The leader, which is always elected on account of his superior height, has his head decorated with tufts of colored woollen fringe, hung with little bells; and his extreme height (often six feet), gallant and graceful carriage, pointed ear, restless eye, and quivering lip, as he faces you for a moment, make him as striking an object as one can well conceive. Upon pressing on him he bounds aside, either up or down the cliff, and is followed by the herd scrambling over places that would be impassable for the mule or the ass.

"They travel immense distances, but by short stages—not more than nine or ten miles per day. It is necessary, in long journeys, to have double the number required to carry the cargo, so as to give them relays. The burden of the llama is about one hundred and thirty pounds; he will not carry more, and will be beat to death rather than move when he is overloaded or tired. The males only are worked; the females are kept for the breed. They appear gentle and docile, but when irritated they have a very savage look, and spit at the object of their anger with great venom. The spittle is said to be very acrid, and will raise blisters where it touches the skin. We saw none in the wild state. They are bred on the haciendas in great numbers. We had no opportunity of seeing the *guanaco* or *alpacca* (other varieties of the Peruvian sheep), though we now and then in crossing the mountains caught a glimpse of the wild and shy *vicuña*. These go in herds of ten or fifteen females, accompanied by one male, who is ever on the alert. On the approach of danger he gives warning by a shrill whistle, and his charge makes off with the speed of the wind. The wool of the vicuña is much finer and more valuable than that of the other species—it is maroon-colored."

Exploration of the Valley of the Amazon *William Lewis Herndon and Lardner Gibbon (Robert Armstrong: Washington, 1854) pp. 54–55.*

Earthquake

Left: the graceful, sturdy llama. The Spanish came to rely on it as much as the Indians traditionally had done.

Below: the H.M.S. *Beagle* near Mount Sarmiento at the beginning of the cruise up the coast of Chile, where Darwin visited the devastated city.

Charles Darwin describes the devastation caused by the great earthquake that shook Chile while he sailed up its coast.

"The earthquake commenced at half-past eleven o'clock in the forenoon. If it had happened in the middle of the night, the greater number of the inhabitants (which in this one province amount to many thousands) must have perished, instead of less than a hundred: as it was, the invariable practice of running out of doors at the first trembling of the ground, alone saved them. In Concepción each house, or row of houses, stood by itself, a heap or line of ruins; but in Talcahuano, owing to the great wave, little more than one layer of bricks, tiles, and timber, with here and there part of a wall left standing, could be distinguished. ... The first shock was very sudden. The mayor-domo at Quiriquina told me, that the first notice he received of it, was finding both the horse he rode and himself, rolling together on the ground. Rising up, he was again thrown down. He also told me that some cows which were standing on the steep side of the island were rolled into the sea. The great wave caused the destruction of many cattle; on one low island, near the head of the bay, seventy animals were washed off and drowned. It is generally thought that this has been the worst earthquake ever recorded in Chile; but as the very severe ones occur only after long intervals, this cannot easily be known; nor indeed would a much worse shock have made any great difference, for the ruin was now complete. Innumerable small tremblings followed the great earthquake, and within the first twelve days no less than three hundred were counted.

"Shortly after the first shock, a great wave was seen from the distance of three or four miles, approaching in the middle of the bay with a smooth outline; but along the shore it tore up cottages and trees, as it swept onwards with irresistible force. At the head of the bay it broke in a fearful line of white breakers, which rushed up to a height of 23 vertical feet above the highest spring-tides. Their force must have been prodigious; for at the Fort a cannon ... estimated at 4 tons in weight, was moved 15 feet inwards. A schooner was left in the midst of the ruins, 200 yards from the beach."

Naturalist's Voyage Round the World *Charles Darwin* (*John Murray: London, 1890*) *pp. 291–293.*

Arrival in a Savage Land

Left: a Pecheray man, one of the Fuegian people described by Darwin.

Right: a Fuegian man, with a family in a primitive hut behind him. Darwin was fascinated by the people.

Armchair travelers in Europe in the 1900's loved tales about the strange peoples and quaint customs explorers met on their journeys. Darwin recounts his first arrival at Tierra del Fuego, at the southernmost tip of South America.

"December 17th, 1832. . . . In the afternoon we anchored in the Bay of Good Success. While entering we were saluted in a manner becoming the inhabitants of this savage land. A group of Fuegians partly concealed by the entangled forest, were perched on a wild point overhanging the sea; and as we passed by, they sprang up and waving their tattered cloaks sent forth a loud and sonorous shout. The savages followed the ship, and just before dark we saw their fire, and again heard their wild cry. . . .

"In the morning the Captain sent a party to communicate with the Fuegians. When we came within hail, one of the four natives who were present advanced to receive us, and began to shout most vehemently, wishing to direct us where to land. When we were on shore the party looked rather alarmed, but continued talking and making gestures with great rapidity. . . . The chief spokesman was old, and appeared to be the head of the family; the three others were powerful young men, about six feet high. The women and children had been sent away. . . . The party altogether closely resembled the devils . . . in plays.

"Their very attitudes were abject, and the expression of their countenances distrustful, surprised, and startled. After we had

Right: a group of Fuegians preparing to leave their cold and frosty land to go on a trading expedition to Patagonia.

presented them with some scarlet cloth, which they immediately tied round their necks, they became good friends. This was shown by the old man patting our breasts, and making a chuckling kind of noise, as people do when feeding chickens. I walked with the old man, and this demonstration of friendship was repeated several times; it was concluded by three hard slaps, which were given me on the breast and back at the same time. He then bared his bosom for me to return the compliment, which being done, he seemed highly pleased. The language of these people, according to our notions, scarcely deserves to be called articulate. Captain Cook has compared it to a man clearing his throat, but certainly no European ever cleared his throat with so many hoarse, guttural, and clicking sounds.

"They are excellent mimics: as often as we coughed or yawned, or made any odd motion, they immediately imitated us. . . . They could repeat with perfect correctness each word in any sentence we addressed them, and they remembered such words for some time. Yet we Europeans all know how difficult it is to distinguish apart the sounds in a foreign language. Which of us, for instance, could follow an American Indian through a sentence of more than three words? All savages appear to possess, to an uncommon degree, this power of mimicry. I was told, almost in the same words, of the same ludicrous habit among the Caffres [Bantus of Africa]."

Naturalist's Voyage Round the World *Charles Darwin (John Murray: London, 1890) pp. 194–196.*

Indian Artifacts

Above: Alfred Wallace. Before he was 20 years old he had already begun making collections of local plants that he found near his home in Wales.

During his travels among the primitive Indians of the Uaupés River, Alfred Wallace made a collection of the many and varied articles they manufactured for everyday use and for special ceremonies. Unfortunately he lost them all on his way home, but his list and drawings of some of them survive. The following is a selection from the 65 types of artifact he noted.

Household Furniture and Utensils
Hammocks, or maqueiras, of palm-fibre, of various materials, colours, and texture.
Small wooden stools, of various sizes, painted and varnished.
Various different shapes and sizes of baskets, made of plaited bark.
Calabashes and gourds, of various shapes and sizes.
Water-pitchers of earthenware.
Pans of earthenware for cooking.
Articles used in the Manufacture of Mandiocca Bread
Mandiocca graters, of quartz fragments set in wood.

Right: an illustration from Wallace's book, showing one of the plantations on the banks of the lower Amazon.

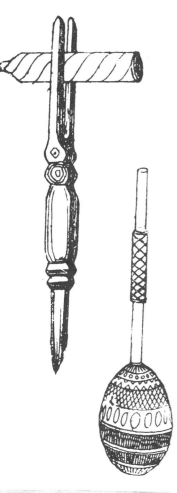

Left: Wallace's drawings of a cigar holder (top) and a rattle used in dancing (bottom). Spruce brought one of the cigar holders back, and it was added to the collection in Kew Gardens.

Tipitis, or wicker elastic pressure cylinders.

Wicker sieves for straining the pulp.

Ovens for roasting cassava-bread and farinha.

Plaited fans for blowing the fire and turning the cakes.

Ornaments, Dress, and Miscellaneous

About twenty distinct articles, forming the feather headdress.

Combs of palm-wood, ornamented with feathers.

Necklaces of seeds and beads.

Bored cylindrical quartz-stone.

Copper earrings, and wooden plugs for the ears.

Armlet of feathers, beads, seeds, etc.

Girdle of jaguars' teeth.

Numbers of cords, made of the "coroá" fibre, mixed with the hair of monkeys and jaguars—making a soft elastic cord used for binding up the hair, and various purposes of ornament.

Painted aprons, or "tangas," made from the inner bark of a tree.

Rattles and ornaments for the legs.

Garters strongly knitted of "coroá."

Packages and carved calabashes, filled with a red pigment called "crajurú."

Large cloths of prepared bark.

Very large carved wooden forks for holding cigars.

Large cigars used at festivals.

Rattles used in dancing, formed of calabashes, carved, and ornamented with small stones inside.

Painted dresses of prepared bark (tururí).

Bottle-shaped baskets, for preserving the edible ants.

Tinder-boxes of bamboo carved, and filled with tinder from an ant's nest.

Small canoe hollowed from a tree.

Paddles used with ditto.

Bark bag, full of sammaúma, the silk-cotton of a *Bombax,* used for making blowing-arrows.

Chest of plaited palm-leaves, used for holding feather-ornaments.

Stone axes, used before the introduction of iron.

Clay cylinders, for supporting cooking utensils.

Travels on the Amazon and Rio Negro *A. R. Wallace (Ward Lock & Co: London, 1889) pp. 350–352.*

A Disastrous Journey

"It is not all pleasure, this exploration" was the understatement of a lifetime from a traveler in Africa in the 1800's. In another unexplored continent, Richard Spruce might well have agreed with him, after the journey described below.

"After a while we began to feel chilly and drowsy; but had we given way to sleep under such circumstances, we might have awaked too stiff to move; to say nothing of the risk of being assaulted by jaguars, which we had been told abounded in the forests. . . . We resumed our march, but the night was cloudy, and scarcely any of the moon's light penetrated the dense forest. However, we scrambled on—now plunging into prickly palms, then getting entangled in sipós, some of which also were prickly. Even by day the sipós are a great obstruction to travelling in the untracked forest; what must they be, then, by night! One's foot trips in a trailing sipó—attempting to withdraw it, one gives the sipó an additional turn, and is perhaps thrown down; or, in stooping to disentangle it, one's chin is caught as in a halter by a stout twisted sipó hanging between two trees. At one time we got on the track of large ants, which crowded on our legs and feet and stung us terribly, and we were many minutes before we could get clear of them. . . .

"The effects of this disastrous journey hung on us for a full week. Besides the rheumatic pains and stiffness brought on by the wetting, our hands, feet, and legs were torn and thickly stuck with prickles, some of which produced ulcers. In comparison . . . the annoyance caused by the bites of ticks large and small and the stings of wasps and ants was trifling and transitory.

"I have been thus minute in my account of this adventure, in order to give some idea of what it is to be lost or benighted in an Amazonian forest. . . . Let the reader try to picture to himself the vast extent of the forest-clad Amazon valley; how few and far between are the habitations of man therein; and how the vegetation is so dense that . . . it is rarely possible to see more than a few paces ahead; so that the lost traveller may be very near to help, or to some known track or landmark, without knowing it. I have heard an Indian, recently established in a new clearing, relate that, having gone out one morning to cut firewood, he had wandered about the whole day before he could find his hut again, although, as he ascertained afterwards, he had never been more than a mile away from it.

"In making one's way though the forest, it is advisable not to cut entirely away the intercepting branches, but to cut or break them half through and bend them forward in the direction of one's route; and this is especially necessary when there are several persons in company, and the turning of a large tree may completely hide the leader from view, although only a few paces ahead. In the excitement of gathering new plants, or of the chase of wild animals, one often forgets to mark the way properly; and it has several times happened to myself, when deep in the forest and quite alone, to be

Above left: the hazards of life in the jungle were as great to the Indians as to the explorers. Here an Indian trying to collect water at the river is attacked by an alligator.

Left: a scene familiar to Spruce—the river, lying ominously still, and in the distance, the all-enveloping jungle.

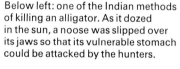

Below left: one of the Indian methods of killing an alligator. As it dozed in the sun, a noose was slipped over its jaws so that its vulnerable stomach could be attacked by the hunters.

unable to find my track when I wished to return along it. It is a rather painful moment when one becomes convinced that the way is irrecoverably lost, and stouter nerves than mine would probably not be entirely unmoved by it. There are no trees all leaning over in the direction of prevailing winds, no mossy side to the trunks, as in the forests of the temperate zones. My plan has been to sit down and patiently watch the sun through the tree-tops until I ascertained his course; then to calculate carefully my own course therefrom, and to follow it unswervingly; by which means I have always come out safely. A pocket-compass is no doubt a very good companion in such emergencies, but it requires to be carried in a waterproof case or pouch, for the bush is almost constantly wet, however clear the sky may be overhead."

Amazon and Andes R. *Spruce* (*Macmillan & Co: London, 1908*) *pp. 94–96.*

India-rubber Trees

Right: Bates kept careful notes on the creatures that he saw. Among those he described was the Jacuaru, a lizard.

The discovery and export of rubber was the cause of a shortlived boom in the prosperity of the towns of the Amazon River Valley. Bates gives an account of the annual collection of rubber by the locals.

"They [the islands of the humid, flat regions of the lower Amazon] are covered with a most luxuriant forest, comprising a large number of indiarubber trees. We found several people encamped here, who were engaged in collecting and preparing the rubber, and thus had an opportunity of observing the process.

"The tree which yields this valuable sap ... belongs ... to a group of plants quite different from that which furnishes the caoutchouc of the East Indies and Africa. This latter is the product of different species of Ficus, and is considered, I believe, in commerce an inferior article to the india-rubber of Pará. The Siphonia elastica grows only on the lowlands in the Amazons region; hitherto the rubber has been collected chiefly in the islands and swampy parts of the mainland within a distance of fifty to a hundred miles to the west of Pará; but there are plenty of untapped trees still growing in the wilds of the Tapajos, Madeira, Juruá, and Jauarí, as far as 1800 miles from the Atlantic coast. The tree is not remarkable in appearance; in bark and foliage it is not unlike the European ash; but the trunk, like that of all forest trees, shoots up to an immense height before throwing off branches. The trees seem to be no man's property hereabout. The people we met with told us they came every year to collect rubber on these islands, as soon as the waters had subsided, namely, in August, and remained till January or February. The process is very simple. Every morning each person, man or woman, to whom is allotted a certain number of trees, goes the round of the whole and collects in a large vessel the milky sap which trickles from gashes made in the bark on the preceding evening, and which is received in little clay cups, or in ampullaria shells stuck beneath the wounds. The sap, which at first is of the consistence of cream, soon thickens; the collectors are provided with a great number of wooden moulds of the shape in which the rubber is wanted, and when they return to the camp they dip them into the liquid, laying on, in the course of several days, one coat after another. When this is done the substance is white and hard; the proper colour and consistency are given by passing it repeatedly through a thick black

Above: a fish that some of the Indians brought to Bates, which they called an Acari fish. It was about a foot long and its body was encased in bony armor.

Right: one of Bates's own drawings of the flat-topped mountains he saw when he was in the lower Amazon region.

smoke obtained by burning the nuts of certain palm trees, after which process the article is ready for sale. India-rubber is known throughout the province only by the name of seringa, the Portuguese word for syringe; it owes this appellation to the circumstance that it was in this form only that the first Portuguese settlers noticed it to be employed by the aborigines. It is said that the Indians were first taught to make syringes of rubber by seeing natural tubes formed by it when the spontaneously-flowing sap gathered round projecting twigs. Brazilians of all classes still use it extensively in the form of syringes, for injections form a great feature in the popular system of cures; the rubber for this purpose is made into a pear-shaped bottle, and a quill fixed in the long neck."

Naturalist on the River Amazons *H. Bates (John Murray: London, 1863) pp. 143–144.*

River Travel on the Amazon

The British naturalist Henry Bates details the common methods of travel on the Amazon River.

Right: an expedition going ashore on the banks of the Amazon. The boat would be pushed along by the poles.

"At the time of my first voyage up the Amazons—namely, in 1849—nearly all communication with the interior was by means of small sailing vessels, owned by traders residing in the remote towns and villages, who seldom came to Pará themselves, but entrusted vessels and cargoes to the care of half-breeds or Portuguese cabos. Sometimes, indeed, they risked all in the hands of the Indian crew, making the pilot, who was also steersman, do duty as supercargo. Now and then, Portuguese and Brazilian merchants at Pará furnished young Portuguese with merchandise, and despatched them to the interior to exchange the goods for produce amongst the scattered population. The means of communication in fact with the upper parts of the Amazons had been on the decrease for some time, on account of the augmented difficulty of obtaining hands to navigate vessels. Formerly, when the Government wished to send any important functionary, such as a judge or a military commandant, into the interior, they equipped a swift-sailing galliota, manned with ten or a dozen Indians. These could travel, on the average, in one day further than the ordinary sailing craft could in three. Indian paddlers were now, however, almost impossible to be obtained, and Government officers were obliged to travel as passengers in trading vessels. The voyage made in this way was tedious in the extreme. When the regular east wind blew—the "vento geral," or trade wind, of the Amazons—sailing vessels could get along very well; but when this failed they were obliged to remain, sometimes many days together, anchored near the shore, or progress laboriously by means of the 'espia.' This latter mode of travelling was as follows. The montaria,

Above right: a bark canoe. Many of the Amazon tribes had developed great skills in using their simple canoes.

Right: a large dugout canoe as used on the Madeira River. These required the collaboration of a well-trained crew.

with twenty or thirty fathoms of cable, one end of which was attached to the foremast, was sent ahead with a couple of hands, who secured the other end of the rope to some strong bough or tree trunk; the crew then hauled the vessel up to the point, after which the men in the boat re-embarked the cable, and paddled forwards to repeat the process. In the dry season, from August to December, when the trade-wind is strong and the currents slack, a schooner could reach the mouth of the Rio Negro, a thousand miles from Pará, in about forty days; but in the wet season, from January to July, when the east wind no longer blows and the Amazons pours forth its full volume of water, flooding the banks and producing a tearing current, it took three months to travel the same distance. It was a great blessing to the inhabitants when, in 1853, a line of steamers was established, and this same journey could be accomplished with ease and comfort, at all seasons, in eight days!"

Naturalist on the River Amazons *H. Bates (John Murray: London, 1863) pp. 22–24.*

An Explorer's Last Letter

Below: Percy Harrison Fawcett, who disappeared without trace while searching for a lost city in the Mato Grosso.

Percy Fawcett's last letter to his wife is reproduced below. He wrote it deep in the Mato Grosso on May 29, 1925, and Indian messengers transported it to the coast. Nothing more was ever heard of Fawcett.

May 29, 1925.

"The attempt to write is fraught with much difficulty owing to the legions of flies that pester one from dawn till dark—and sometimes all through the night! The worst are the tiny ones smaller than a pinhead, almost invisible, but stinging like a mosquito. Clouds of them are always present. Millions of bees add to the plague, and other bugs galore. The stinging horrors get all over one's hands, and madden. Even the head nets won't keep them out. As for mosquito nets, the pests fly through them!

"We hope to get through this region in a few days, and are

camped here for a couple of days to arrange for the return of the *peons,* who are anxious to get back, having had enough of it—and I don't blame them. We go on with eight animals—three saddle mules, four cargo mules, and a *madrinha,* a leading animal which keeps the others together. Jack is well and fit, getting stronger every day even though he suffers a bit from the insects. I myself am bitten or stung by ticks, and these *piums,* as they call the tiny ones, all over the body. Raleigh I am anxious about. He still has one leg in a bandage, but won't go back. So far we have plenty of food, and no need to walk, but I am not sure how long this will last. There may be so little for the animals to eat. I cannot hope to stand up to this journey better than Jack or Raleigh, but I had to do it. Years tell, in spite of the spirit of enthusiasm.

"I calculate to contact the Indians in about a week or ten days, when we should be able to reach the waterfall so much talked about.

"Here we are at Dead Horse Camp, Lat. 11° 43′ S. and 54° 35′ W., the spot where my horse died in 1920. Only his white bones remain. We can bathe ourselves here, but the insects make it a matter of great haste. Nevertheless, the season is good. It is *very cold* at night, and fresh in the morning; but insects and heat come by mid-day, and from then till six o'clock in the evening it is sheer misery in camp.

"You need have no fear of any failure . . ."

Exploration Fawcett *P. H. Fawcett (Hutchinson: London, 1953).*

Below: one of Fawcett's encounters with the primitive Amazonian Indians, as visualized in this drawing by his only surviving son, Brian.

Below right: a photograph of Fawcett (second from the left) in the jungle on one of his early survey parties.

The Explorers

ACUNA, CRISTOBAL DE
1597(?)–1676   Spain
1637–1639: Accompanied Pedro
Teizeira on an exploratory trip down
the Amazon River.

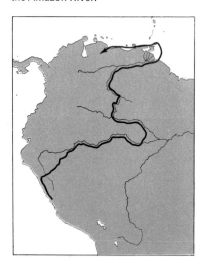

AGUIRRE, LOPE DE
1508(?)–1561   Spain
1559: Joined expedition led by Pedro
de Urzūa to search for El Dorado.
1561: Murdered leader and his
successor and took control of
expedition himself. Plundered
Indian villages.

ALMAGRO, DIEGO DE
1475(?)–1538   Spain
1524–1525: Accompanied Francisco
Pizarro on his first attempt to

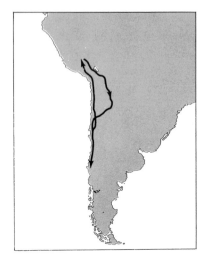

find the Inca empire. Explored the
coast of Colombia. Returned to
Panama without reaching Peru.
1526: Took part in second voyage
to Peru. After two return trips
to Panama to replenish troops and
supplies, they reached the Inca
city of Tumbes, in the Gulf of
Guayaquil, present-day Ecuador.
1531–1533: Took part in conquest of
Peru, joining Pizarro's expedition
at Cajamarca.
1535–1536: Conquered Chile, led expedition south from Cusco along the
shores of Lake Titicaca into present-
day Bolivia and Argentina. Crossed
the Chilean Andes and reached the
port of Copiapó. Continued south as
far as present-day Santiago. Sent
small party to the south before returning to Peru along the coast.
Became the first white man to cross
the forbidding Atacama Desert in
northern Chile.
See map on pages 38–39

BATES, HENRY WALTER
1852–1892   Britain
1848: With Wallace he went to Pará in
South America and up the Tocantins
River. He journeyed up the Amazon to
Manaus, then to Ega, where he stayed
for a year before returning to Pará.
1851–1855: Based at Santarém, then

went up the Amazon to Ega, where he
spent the next four years collecting.
1859: Sailed home to England, which
he reached after a journey which lasted
for nearly two years.
See map on pages 146–147

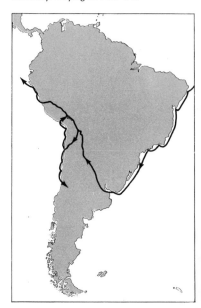

BINGHAM, HIRAM
1875–1956   United States
1906–1924: Made six expeditions to
South America.
1911: Discovered the "lost city" of
the Inca, Machu Picchu, high in the
Peruvian Andes.

BONPLAND, AIMÉ
1773–1858   France
1799–1804: Traveled to South America
with Alexander von Humboldt, made
scientific research expeditions to
Cuba, Mexico, the Andes, and
elsewhere.
1818–1821: Professor in Buenos Aires.
1821–1830: Imprisoned in Paraguay.
See map on pages 76–77

CABOT, JOHN
1450–1498:   Venice
1497: In the service of England
sailed west in search of Asia.
Reached Cape Breton island (off the

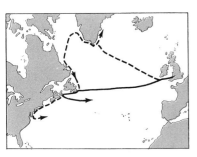

coast of Nova Scotia) and Newfoundland, convinced he had reached the shores of Asia.
1498: Explored the east and west coasts of Greenland, sailed south along the shores of Labrador to Nova Scotia and then continued sailing south along the coast, possibly reaching Delaware Bay.

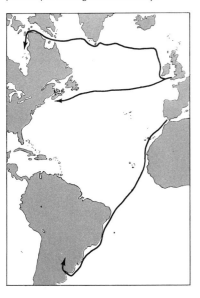

CABOT, SEBASTIAN
1474–1557   Venice
1497: Accompanied his father on the expedition to Nova Scotia and Newfoundland.
1509: Sailed as far as Hudson Bay in search of a northwest passage.
1526: Visited Paraguay and the Rio de la Plata in South America.

CABRAL, PEDRO ÁLVARES
1467–1519   Portugal
1500: Appointed by King Manuel I to command a large, well-armed and heavily laden fleet bound for India on Portugal's first major trading mission to the East. Swept westward through the Atlantic on the way, and discovered Brazil. In India was successful in making treaties with the ruler of Cochin and Cannanore. Returned home in 1501, his ships laden with valuable commodities from Eastern markets.
See map on pages 38–39

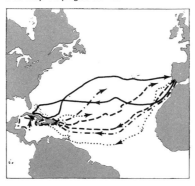

COLUMBUS, CHRISTOPHER
1451–1506   Genoa
1492: Sailed west in the service of Spain in search of the Indies. Discovered San Salvador, Cuba and Hispaniola, although to the end of his life he believed he had reached the Orient.
1493: On his second voyage west, dis-

covered Dominica, Guadeloupe, and Mariagalante, and sighted the Virgin Islands. Set up a colony at Hispaniola.
1498: On his third voyage across the Atlantic, discovered Trinidad and sighted the coast of South America (which he mistook for another island). Traveled on to Hispaniola.
1500: Was arrested and divested of position as governor of Hispaniola.
1502: Final voyage west. Forbidden to revisit Hispaniola, he traveled down the coast of Central America.

CORTES, HERNANDO
1485–1547   Spain
1504: Went to Santo Domingo in the West Indies.
1511: Took part in Velásquez's conquest of Cuba.

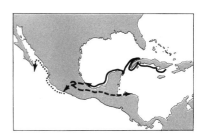

1519: Commissioned by Velásquez to lead an expedition to conquer Mexico. Sailed from Cuba to Cozumel Island off the coast of Yucatán. Then followed the coast to the island of San Juan de Ulua. He founded the city of Veracruz, the first colony in New Spain. Marched inland, through Tlaxacala where he made allies of the local Indians.
Crossing the Sierra Madre Mountains, he reached the Aztec city of Tenochtitlán, captured the emperor Montezuma, and established Spanish control. While on the coast, the Aztec rose up against the Spanish. Cortes was unable to crush the rebellion and he and his men were forced to flee the capital.
1521: Laid siege to Tenochtitlán and destroyed the city. Founded the capital of New Spain, Mexico City, on its ruins.
1524–1525: Led an expedition into

Honduras, where he executed the rebel Olid and secured the territory for Spain.
1534: Commanded an expedition that founded the first Spanish colony in Lower California.

DARWIN, CHARLES
1809–1882   England
1831: He sailed from England for South America. Visited the islands of Rocas, and Fernando de Noronha. He called at Rio de Janeiro and then traveled a short distance inland. Next he went to the Rio de la Plata and sailed down the coast, making extensive journeys inland up the Paraná and Colorado rivers and then on to Bahía Blanca. He visited the Patagonian coast, Tierra del Fuego, and the Falkland Islands, sailed through the Strait of Magellan and also around Cape Horn. He next sailed up the west coast as far as Lima, calling at various places and making one inland journey in Chile. He also visited the Galápagos Islands and returned home across the Pacific, thus completing a voyage around the world.
See map on page 100

FAWCETT, PERCY HARRISON
1867–1925   England
1906: Explored in the region of the boundary of Bolivia and Brazil, the Verde River, and the Mato Grosso.
1913: He went to Cuyaba (near the headwaters of the Paraguay River) and explored the Mato Grosso and the Xingú River area.
1925: Lost without trace in Mato Grosso or Xingú area.
See map on pages 146–147

HUMBOLDT, ALEXANDER VON
1769–1859   Germany
1799: Sailed from Europe to the mouth of the Orinoco, went upriver and proved that it was linked with the Amazon, via the Negro, by a natural canal, now named the Casiquiare.
1800: Traveled to Cuba, crossed south to Cartagena, went up the Magdalena River and visited Quito, Lima, and the sources of the Amazon.

1803: Went to Acapulco on the west coast of Mexico, then to Mexico City. Made excursions to Guanajuata, and Jalapa. Sailed home from Veracruz, calling at Philadelphia.
1829: Accompanied by Rose and Ehrenberg, went to Moscow and then to Perm (Molotov). Visited Tobolsk, went to the Ob River, and south to the Altai Mountains. Returned to Moscow via Omsk, down the Volga to the Caspian, and up the Don.
See map on pages 76–77

JIMENÉZ DE QUESADA, GONZALO
1497(?)–1579   Spain
1536: Set out to explore the interior of Colombia in search of the kingdom of El Dorado. Explored the Magdalena, Colombia's chief river. Reached the high plains of the central Colombian Andes— home of the Chibcha Indians. Conquered the Chibcha in 1538, and founded Bogotá, the capital of modern Bolivia.
See map on pages 38–39

LA CONDAMINE, CHARLES
1771–1774   France
1736: Went on a scientific expedition to Peru (which then extended north to the equator).
1743: He left Quito for France, went down into the Amazon basin to the Marañón River and down the Amazon as far as Manaus. Then he went part way up the Negro River. He continued down the Amazon to Pará. He left for French Guiana and coasted the island of Marajo, passed northward to Guiana. Sailed from Paramaribo to Holland, and then to Paris.
See map on pages 76–77

MAGELLAN, FERDINAND
1480(?)–1521   Portugal
1505: Sailed to India in the great armada of Francisco de Almeida.
1509: Took part in the naval battle against the Moors at Diu. Sailed in first Portuguese expedition to Malaya.
1511: Took part in first Portuguese expedition to Moluccas.

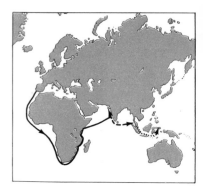

1519: Set out in service of Spain to find a westward route to India. After touching in at Rio de Janeiro Bay, and stopping at several other points along the coast east of South America, found the strait leading from the Atlantic to the Pacific.

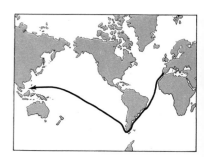

Sailed as far as the Philippines where he was killed in a battle with the natives of Mactan.

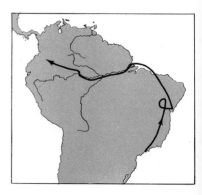

MARTIUS, KARL FRIEDRICK PHILIPP VON
1794–1868   Germany
1817: Traveled on naturalist expedition to Brazil.
See map at bottom of previous column

ORELLANA, FRANCISCO DE
1500(?)–1550(?)   Spain
1541: Served under Gonzalo Pizarro
in his expedition to the east of
Peru in search of the kingdom of
El Dorado. Continued journey by
boat down the Napo and Cocoa rivers
to the valley of the Amazon. Explored the course of the Amazon from
the Andes Mountains to the Atlantic.
See map on pages 38–39

PINZÓN, VINCENTE
1460(?)–1524(?)   Spain
1492: Sailed as captain of the
Niña on Columbus's first voyage
across the Atlantic.
1499–1500: Sailed west across the
Atlantic to Cape St. Roque on the
eastern bulge of South America.
From here, sailed northwest along
the coast to the mouth of the
Amazon, and then to Costa Rica.
1508: Further explored the east
coast of South America in search
of a southwest passage to the Indies.
See map on pages 38–39

PIZARRO, FRANCISCO
1478(?)–1541   Spain
1502: Arrived at the island of Hispaniola.
1524: Set out on his first attempt to
reach Peru. Sailed as far as the coast
of Colombia, where he explored the
coast.
1526: With Bartolome de la Ruiz as
captain, sailed to the Colombian
coast. Led a plundering expedition
inland, while Almagro returned to
Panama and Ruiz sailed farther south.
Spent some time on the island of
Gallo off the coast of Ecuador awaiting reinforcements. Then sailed south
to the Inca city of Tumbes before
returning to Panama.
1531–1532: Sailed from Panama to
conquer Peru. Began his campaign
from the city of Tumbes. Founded

the city of San Miguel before advancing to Cajamarca and defeating
the Inca emperor.
1533: With reinforcements brought
by Almagro, marched from Cajamarca
to the Inca capital of Cusco high
in the Andes.
1535: Founded the city of Lima on
the banks of the Rimac River.
See map on pages 38–39

PIZARRO, GONZALO
1506(?)–1548   Spain
1531–1532: Accompanied his brother
in the conquest of the Inca empire.
1541: Led an expedition into north-
western South America in search of
the kingdom of El Dorado. Set out
from Quito in present-day Ecuador
and crossing the eastern Cordillera
of the Andes descended into the
jungle growth of the Amazon basin.
Reached the banks of the Cocoa River
and followed it to its junction with
the Napo. Abandoned by Orellana,
he and his men were forced to fight
their way back to Quito without
supplies or weapons.
See map on pages 38–39

RALEIGH, WALTER
1552(?)–1618   England
1585: His first colonizing expedition
left Plymouth, England, and established
colony on Roanoke Island in Pamlico
Sound. Colony failed and settlers
returned to England in 1586.
1587: Second attempt to colonize
Roanoke.
1595: Led expedition to Guiana in
South America to search for El Dorado,
the legendary land of gold. The
expedition failed.
1616: Final expedition again to search
for gold in South America. Raleigh's
men attacked the Spaniards, against
express orders of King James I, and the
project had to be abandoned.
1618: Executed by king's order.
See map on pages 38–39

ROOSEVELT, THEODORE
1858–1919   United States
1913–1914: Explored the Duvido
River in the Brazilian jungle, traveling
from its mouth to source. His company

included his son Kermit, George Cherrie,
and Colonel Candido Rondon.
See map on pages 146–147

VESPUCCI, AMERIGO
1451–1512   Florence
1499: Sailed with Alonso de Ojeda,
exploring north coast of South

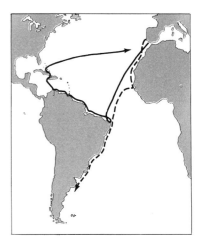

America from Cape St. Roque, Brazil,
to Gulf of Venezuela.
1501: Sailed, in the service of
Portugal, to the coast of South
America, and, although his claims
to having traveled as far south as
latitude 50°S are not now believed,
it is considered quite probable
that he did travel as far south as
latitude 32°S.

WALLACE, ALFRED RUSSEL
1823–1913   Britain
1848: With Bates, arrived at Pará,
then went up the Tocantins River and
up the Amazon to Manaus. From here
Wallace continued up the Negro,
explored up the Uaupes as far as
the second cataract at Juaurite.
He came down the Uaupes, continued
up the Negro, crossed over to the
Orinoco, went down the river, and
returned to England.
1854–1860: He explored in the
East Indies Archipelago including
New Guinea.
See map on pages 146–147

Glossary

Amazon women: In Greek mythology, a race of female warriors who fought with the ancient Greeks and made slaves of the men they conquered. A similar Indian myth tells of a tribe of female warriors in South America. In both cases the legend may have derived from mistaking long-haired men for women.

Araucanians: Members of a large Indian group in Chile, famed for their long and successful resistance to the invading Spaniards. Araucanians originally occupied coastal Chile, but began to move into Argentina in the 1500's, using horses taken from the Spaniards. They were defeated by an Argentine army in 1879, and by Chilean forces in 1883. Today there are about 300,000 Araucanians in South America, most of them farmers.

Aztec: Members of one of the most civilized and powerful Indian groups in ancient America. They occupied the Valley of Mexico and regions around it for more than 300 years until Hernando Cortes' Spanish troops conquered them in 1521. The Aztec were famous as warriors, and had a highly developed and efficient military organization. The basis of their highly advanced culture was their complex religion. Large-scale human sacrifice was a negative feature of that religion.

bandito: Half-breed outlaw. Armed with razor-sharp knives, these men roamed the interior of Brazil, attacking ranchers and travelers.

bore: A tidal flood. Such tides occur in shallow river mouths and bays where there is a wide range between low and high tides, and the incoming tide builds up into a high wall.

bowsprit: A large spar projecting forward from the bow of a ship

brigantine: A two-masted square-rigged ship. It differed from a brig, which was also two-masted, in that it did not have a square mainsail.

bubonic plague: Plague in which there is inflammatory swelling of the lymph glands, especially in the groin.

One of the worst of all epidemic diseases, it has a very high death rate. In the 1300's a form of bubonic plague known as the black death destroyed one fourth of the population of Europe.

caballero: Spanish word for a knight, a cavalier, a horseman, or a member of the Spanish lower nobility. Military service in the colonies was often the only chance a caballero had to win riches, status, and adventure.

capybara: A tailless, largely aquatic, South American rodent. It is the largest rodent in the world, often exceeding 4 feet in length.

caymans: Any of several Central and South American reptiles, similar to alligators but often resembling crocodiles in appearance.

Chibcha: Indian tribe living on the high plains of the Colombian Andes. They lived in small villages, worked gold, drilled emeralds, made pottery and wove textiles. Hundreds of the Chibcha were slaughtered and tortured by a contingent of Spanish troops led by Gonzalo Jiménez de Quesada.

chigger: A six-legged larval mite that sucks the blood of vertebrates, causing intense irritation to the victim.

cinnamon: Highly aromatic and pleasantly flavored spice. Made from the bark of any of several trees of the laurel family. A valued luxury in the Middle Ages.

conquistadors: A Spanish word meaning conquerors. Specifically used for leaders in the Spanish conquest of America, and especially Mexico and Peru, in the 1500's.

curare: Deadly poison used by South American Indian tribesmen to smear on tips of their arrows. Sometimes also called oorara, oorari or urari. Curare is made from various poisonous plants found in the South American jungles. The poison is powerful only when injected into the blood stream or outer tissues of the body, where it paralyzes the muscles. Curare has been used in the treatment of tetanus and hydro-

phobia, and is also sometimes used during anesthesia to cause relaxation of the muscles so as to permit the use of smaller doses of anesthetic.

Cusco: Capital of the Inca Empire, captured by Francisco Pizarro in 1533. Cusco, in southern Peru, is now a trading center for local farmers.

El Dorado: A city or country of fabulous riches believed by early explorers to exist somewhere in South America. Supposed to be ruled by a king also named El Dorado, the gilded one, because he was said to anoint himself with gold dust. The name is used nowadays to denote a place of fabulous wealth.

gaucho: Cowboy of the South American pampas. Gauchos played an important part in the development of Argentina and Uruguay. They were usually of mixed Spanish and Indian descent. They were very skillful riders and spent most of their time on horse-back. The coming of refrigerated ships led to the development of the meat industry, which made cattle ranching big business, and so ended the gaucho's way of life.

geodesy: The branch of applied mathematics that determines the exact positions and the figures and areas of large portions of the earth's surface, the shape and size of the earth, and the variations of terrestrial gravity and magnetism.

Gran Chaco: Thinly populated, swampy region of south central South America. Drained by the Paraguay River and its chief western tributaries.

grandee: Man of elevated rank or station, especially a Spanish or Portuguese nobleman of the first rank.

guano: Waste matter of sea birds and bats. Makes valuable fertilizer because it is rich in nitrate and phosphate. Islands off Peru have long been the main source of supply. Deposits there once covered the surface to a depth of more than 100 feet.

hidalgo: Member of the Spanish

lower nobility. With caballeros, hidalgos made up the majority of the Spanish conquistadors.

Inca: Before the coming of the white man, Inca Indians had developed a mighty and civilized empire in South America. At its peak, from A.D. 1450 to 1532, the empire stretched more than 2,500 miles from north to south. Its population was between $3\frac{1}{2}$ million and 7 million. There were good communications, well organized armies and a strong political and social system. The Inca were only conquered by the Spaniards, after years of fighting, because the invaders had the advantages of firearms, horses, and steel armor.

llama: The largest member of the camel family that lives in South America. The llama has no hump, and is 4 or 5 feet tall at the shoulder, and about 4 or 5 feet long in the body. Males are used by Indians of the South American Andes as pack animals, females for breeding and furs. The llama can carry about 100 pounds in weight and can travel between 15 and 20 miles a day with a full load.

Machu Picchu: Site of an ancient Inca city on a mountain in the Andes, northwest of Cusco, Peru. Ruins include a temple and a citadel surrounded by terraced gardens. Discovered by Hiram Bingham in 1911.

malaria: Human disease caused by parasites in the red blood cells. Transmitted by the bite of Anopheles mosquitoes and characterized by periodic attacks of chills and fever.

mangrove trees: Tropical maritime trees or shrubs that throw out many prop roots and form dense masses.

manioc roots: Plants of the cassava family, grown in the tropics for their fleshy, edible rootstock, which yields nutritious starch.

meridian: Great imaginary circle on the surface of the earth passing through the poles and any given place.

Mato Grosso: State in western Brazil in center of great forest area.

natural selection: Natural process tending to cause the survival of individuals or groups best adjusted to the conditions under which they live. Equally important for perpetuation of desirable genetic quantities and elimination of undesirable ones.

Noble Savage: In the 1700's, the French writer Jean-Jacques Rousseau advocated a return to nature. He claimed that the evils of humanity came from civilization, and regarded primitive man as the *Noble Savage*. His school of thought gained great popularity for a time.

pampa: Spanish word meaning plain, used for several extensive, generally grass-covered plains of South America. Most commonly refers to the huge plain in central South America. During the wet season the pampa has a thick growth of grass and makes excellent pasture for sheep and cattle. Has recently been developed more and more for farming.

piranha (also known as caribi): Small voracious fish of the Amazon River. Considered by some scientists more dangerous than sharks. Piranhas range from 4 to 18 inches long. They attack in large numbers and have been known to tear all the flesh from a human or animal skeleton in a few minutes.

Quetzalcoatl: Aztec god. One of the beliefs of the Aztec religion was that the god, who was fair skinned and bearded, had gone on a long journey by sea, and would one day return to Tenochtitlán, the Aztec capital. When he heard of the advancing Spanish troops, Montezuma II convinced himself that these were Quetzalcoatl and his allies and allowed them to come into his capital without hindering them in any way.

quinine: A substance from the bark of cinchona trees found in South America. Quinine is used to treat malaria and other diseases. In malaria it reduces the fever during attacks but does not cure the disease. In many tropical areas quinine is cheap and easy to obtain.

rain forest: Tropical woodland with annual rainfall of at least 100 inches. It is marked by lofty, broad, curved evergreen trees, shrubs, and creeping vines that form a continuous canopy.

rotenone: Crystalline insecticide harmless to warm-blooded animals. Used especially in private gardens.

savannas: Tropical or subtropical grasslands containing scattered trees and drought-resistant undergrowth.

selva: Thickly forested plain of the Amazon Valley in South America. Often called rain forest. Plant life includes trees such as rubber, bamboo, rosewood, Brazil nut, cacao, and wax palm. There are thick tangles of tropical plants among the trees.

social caste: Division of society based upon difference of wealth, inherited rank or privilege, profession or occupation.

Tenochtitlán: Capital of the Aztec Empire. Called by Cortes "The Venice of the New World." It was built up on the shallow waters of Lake Texcoco, and connected to the mainland by earthen causeways with drawbridges. Aqueducts carried water into the city from a nearby hill. A main ceremonial plaza in the center of the city was the site of numbers of temples dedicated to principal Aztec gods.

triangulation: A technique used to survey, measure, and map a geographical area by dividing it into triangles and measuring the bases and angles that are formed.

tsunami: Japanese word for *storm wave*. A great sea wave caused by submarine earthquake or volcanic eruption.

vampire bat: Any of several large or small South and Central American bats reputed to feed on the blood of insects and humans.

viceroy: Governor of country or province who rules as representative of his king or sovereign.

white water: Frothy water, as in breakers, rapids, or waterfalls.

Index

Picture Credits

Listed below are the sources of all the illustrations in this book. To identify the source of a particular illustration, first find the relevant page on the diagram opposite. The number in black in the appropriate position on that page refers to the credit as listed below.

1 Aldus Archives
2 The Bettmann Archive
3 Bibliothèque de Ministère/Photo Giraudon
4 Reproduced by permission of the Trustees of the British Museum
5 British Museum/Photo R. B. Fleming © Aldus Books
6 Trustees of the British Museum (Natural History)/Photo Mike Busselle © Aldus Books
7 Photo Mike Busselle © Aldus Books
8 Harald Schultz/Bruce Coleman Ltd.
9 James Simon/Bruce Coleman Ltd.
10 *Daily Telegraph* Colour Library
11 Down House Collection/Photo © George Rainbird Ltd., 1969
12 Mary Evans Picture Library
13 From a drawing by Brian Fawcett
14 Photo Brian Fawcett
15 Photo P. H. Fawcett
16 © Geographical Projects Limited, London
17 Photo Giraudon
18 Michael Holford Library
19 The John Judkyn Memorial, Freshford Manor, Bath/Photo Mike Busselle © Aldus Books
20 Mansell/Alinari
21 Mansell Collection
22 Photo Mas, Barcelona
23 Collection Mauritshuis, The Hague /Photo A. J. M. van der Vaart
24 John H. Moore
25 Museo Nacional de Historia, Madrid/Photo Pulido Gudino
26 Museo Navale, Madrid/Photo © George Rainbird Ltd., 1969
27 National Maritime Museum, Greenwich/Photo © George Rainbird Ltd., 1969
28 National Portrait Gallery, London
29 Roger Perry
30 Photo-Library Inc.
31 Picturepoint, London
32 Mauro Pucciarelli, Rome
33 Radio Times Hulton Picture Library
34 Photo © George Rainbird Ltd., 1969
35 Collection Roger-Viollet, Paris
36 Photo © George Rainbird Ltd., 1969, reproduced by courtesy of the Royal College of Surgeons of England
37 Photo John Webb © Aldus Books, reproduced by permossion of the Royal Geographical Society
38 Mr. Simon Wingfield Digby, Sherborne Castle
39 David St. Clair, *The Mighty, Mighty Amazon,* Souvenir Press, London, 1968

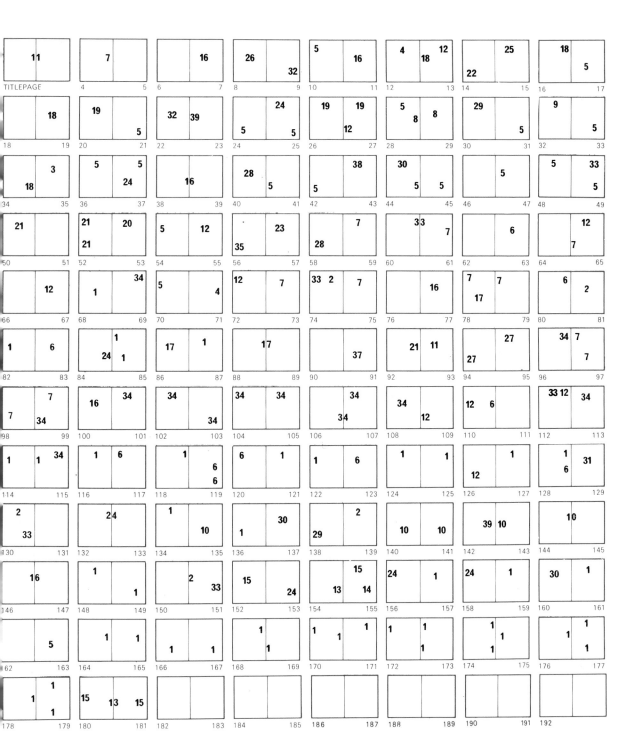